BEHIND

THE

DREAM

To: Ned —
My very best
wishes
14 Jan JoB

BEHIND
THE
DREAM

THE MAKING OF

THE SPEECH

THAT TRANSFORMED

A NATION

CLARENCE B.

JONES

AND

STUART CONNELLY

palgrave
macmillan

First published in hardcover in 2011 by PALGRAVE MACMILLAN® in the US—
a division of St. Martin's Press LLC, 175 Fifth Avenue, New York, NY 10010.

Where this book is distributed in the UK, Europe and the rest of the world, this is
by Palgrave Macmillan, a division of Macmillan Publishers Limited, registered in
England, company number 785998, of Houndmills, Basingstoke, Hampshire RG21
6XS.

Palgrave Macmillan is the global academic imprint of the above companies and has
companies and representatives throughout the world.

Palgrave® and Macmillan® are registered trademarks in the United States, the
United Kingdom, Europe and other countries.

ISBN: 978-0-230-33755-8

The Library of Congress has catalogued the hardcover edition as follows:
Jones, Clarence B.
    Behind the dream : the making of the speech that transformed a nation / Clarence
B. Jones and Stuart Connelly.
        p.   cm.
    ISBN 978-0-230-10368-9
    1. King, Martin Luther, Jr., 1929–1968. I have a dream.   2. King, Martin
Luther, Jr., 1929–1968—Influence.   3. March on Washington for Jobs and Free-
dom, Washington, D.C., 1963.   4. Speeches, addresses, etc., American—Wash-
ington (D.C.)   5. African Americans—Civil rights—History—20th century.
6. Civil rights movements—United States—History—20th century.   I. Connelly,
Stuart.   II. Title.
E185.97.K5J576   2010
323.092—dc22

                                                                        2010021207

A catalogue record of the book is available from the British Library.

Design by Letra Libre

First PALGRAVE MACMILLAN paperback edition: March 2012

10 9 8 7 6 5 4 3 2 1

Printed in the United States of America.

A chauffeur brings you to your destination
A gardener helps living things grow
A cook nourishes your body
A maid takes your burdens from you
And a nun brings God to your eyes, ears, lips

If I have lived anything beyond an ordinary life,
it is only by the love and guiding wisdom of
Goldsborough, Mary, and Sister Mary Patricia

—*Clarence B. Jones*

I was born on August 30, 1964, one year and two days after
the March on Washington. My twins were born in 2003.

But all three of us were born in a new American century.

For that, we owe a debt of gratitude to those who toiled in
the Civil Rights Movement and forced this country to live
up to her ideals.

For Callie, Wesley, and my loving wife, Mary Jo.

—*Stuart Connelly*

CONTENTS

PROLOGUE

SOULS BEYOND
MEASURE

Reverend KING stated that he had mixed emotions about President KENNEDY in that the President should be made to know that "we" are not satisfied with him and what he has done to the field of civil rights . . .

—Excerpt from illegal wiretap authorized by
J. Edgar Hoover, Director,
Federal Bureau of Investigation

This now-declassified report, along with the others referenced in this book, remains cataloged by the FBI under the heading

NEGRO QUESTION

A quarter of a million people, human beings who generally had spent their lives treated as something less, stood shoulder to shoulder across that vast lawn, their hearts beating as one. Hope on the line. When hope was an increasingly scarce resource.

There is no dearth of prose describing the mass of humanity that made its way to the feet of the Great Emancipator that day; no metaphor that has slipped through the cracks waiting to be discovered, dusted off, and injected into the discourse a half century on. The March on Washington has been compared to a tsunami, a shockwave, a wall, a living monument, a human mosaic, an outright miracle.

It was all of those things, and if you saw it with your own eyes, it wasn't hard to write about. With that many people in one place crying out for something so elemental, you don't have to be Robert Frost to offer some profound eloquence.

Still, I can say to those who know the event only as a steely black-and-white television image, it's a shame that the colors of that day—the blue sky, the vibrant green life, the golden sun everywhere—are not part of our national memory. There is something heart-wrenching about the widely shown images and film clips of the event that belies the joy of the day. But it could be worse. We could have been marching in an era before cameras and recording devices; then the specifics of the event would eventually fade out of living memory and the world would be left only with the mythology and the text. Text without context, in this case especially, would be quite a loss. One might imagine standing before an audience and reading Reverend Martin Luther King, Jr.'s "I Have a Dream" speech verbatim, but it is a stretch to believe that any such performance would sow the seeds of change with, as Dr. King put it that day in Washington, the "fierce urgency of now." The vast crowd, the great speaker, the words that shook the world—it all comes as a package deal. We are truly fortunate to have a record. Yet what the television cameras and radio microphones captured that August day is but a sliver of the vibrancy of the event. When a film adaptation of a beloved novel premieres, the people who say "Oh, but you've got to read the book" are inevitably right. The density of the written word makes the flat motion picture a pale artifact in comparison. In a similar fashion, although watching the black-and-white news footage of Dr. King's historic call to action is stirring to almost everyone who sees it, learning about the work that went into The March and the speech—the discussions and debates behind closed doors—offers a unique context that magnifies the resonance of hearing those famous words "I have a dream" in that phenomenal, inimitable cadence.

If, taken together, the images and recordings of Martin make up that "movie" of the 1963 March on Washington in our collective consciousness, and if it's true, as people often say, that "If you loved the movie, you've got to read the book," *Behind the Dream* is that book. It is a story not known to the general public or disclosed to participants in The March—or, in fact, to many of its organizers. I acquired private truths and quiet insights during the months leading up to this historic event. For the most part, I've kept them to myself. But as this book is published, I will be entering my ninth decade on this Earth, and as I move closer to the final horizon, I realize the time has come to share what I know. The experiences cannot die with me; the full truth is simply too important to history.

For those of us who put The March together, several aspects of that day struck a chord and went on to have a profound effect on us. First was the most obvious—the size of the crowd. It was truly staggering. Estimates vary widely, depending on the agenda of who was keeping count, but those of us who were involved in planning The March put the number at a minimum of 250,000. They showed up to connect with The Movement, to draw strength from the speakers and from each other. This was perhaps not so surprising, since the underpinning of the Civil Rights Movement had always been our sense of communal strength. It is in part why the Black Church was a focal point for The Movement; it allowed individuals to see that they were not alone in their suffering, their loss of dignity, their humiliation. But congregations were measured in the hundreds of families, not hundreds of *thousands*. The March was an especially important milestone for African Americans because it allowed many who suffered the degradation and sometimes physical abuse of racism in relative isolation to share with a vast number of people their pain as well as their hope and optimism for a better day.

A kind of unique energy emanated from the massive crowd, and it was just that energy that made the words in Martin Luther King, Jr.'s speech resonate. He had, in fact, used the phrase "I have a dream" in a previous speech with hardly anyone registering anything exceptional about it. It played out differently that August day. The reason is simple: The power is not in the words themselves. Nor is it in the speaker. The power was woven into the feedback loop that jumped between the words, the speaker, and his audience. It was those quarter of a million souls who made the "dream" the "*Dream.*" It was a perfect storm. I know, because I saw it happen. I was standing no more than fifty feet behind Martin when I saw Mahalia Jackson, his favorite gospel singer, look to him with a beaming face and shout a piece of advice. As the suggestion took root, I watched Martin push aside the text of the speech I'd helped prepare—a text, it bears noting, that *did not* contain the phrase "I have a dream."

At that moment I looked to the person standing next to me. "These people out there today don't know it yet," I said, "but they're about ready to go to church."

Something else the organizers became aware of, more surprising than the size of the crowd, was its diversity in age.

Naturally we had expected college students, even some high school students, but there were little children, septuagenarians, and everything in between. It was exhilarating to see the generations come together over such an important issue. Even those who *knew* they would never live to see the needle budge a millimeter in favor of Negroes, let alone make it to "the Promised Land," were there, fighting for those on down the line. This was one important key to The Movement, out in the open but invisible to most who opposed us: It was never about *me now,* it was always about *someone someday.* It could not have worked otherwise.

Less satisfying was the lack of racial diversity at The March. We knew well how much support we had within the white community and had anticipated greater white participation. Our hopes were that non-Negro turnout would tip the scales at 30 percent or perhaps even higher. Granted, our methods of calculation were crude at best, but the general consensus among The March organizers was that actual non-Negro turnout was no more than 20 percent. This was a disappointment, especially to Martin. I still have no explanation for the number, other than the tried-and-true notion that everyone in Hollywood and Washington knows by heart: It's easier to write a check for the charity banquet than to show up to eat.

Finally, in the days and weeks after the event, we organizers were continually surprised at how often Dr. King's speech was replayed and rebroadcast. It was on television constantly, and several independent record companies churned out hastily made albums of the speech, which flew off the shelves. That is, of course, until we put them out of business. Those companies thought they were selling something that was in the public domain, where political speeches almost always reside, but on August 28, 1963, I had changed the rules. I claim no great foresight in this matter. On a whim, I had done something no one had ever thought to do in the history of political discourse: I had copyrighted the speech that morning. It was a relatively simple act, an afterthought. It was done merely as a way to confound those who might take advantage of my friend Martin. I had seen that happen many times before, and, as his lawyer, I wanted to protect him. I never imagined the intellectual ownership of "I Have a Dream" would prove to be a kind of endless financial river, generating substantial sums of money year after year to fund Dr. King's ongoing work through the King Center.

Martin was taken from us far too early, of course, but sometimes I look at that miracle of economics and I am tempted to think, "Yeah, revenge certainly is a dish best served cold." But Martin was far too noble a man to ever use a coarse word like "revenge," and though I am not speaking for him here, I should be respectful as to how he surely would want me to present the situation. Simply stated: There is sweet justice in the fact that, though his voice may have been silenced, it is literally that same voice echoing from beyond the grave that provides funds to this day for his great work. The Lord indeed works in mysterious ways.

But these assessments were all made after the fact, more a kind of civil rights Monday-morning quarterbacking than visceral experience of the day itself. And it is that visceral experience I want to share with you in these pages. I saw history unfold in a way no one else could have, from behind the scenes. And now it's time to give those personal experiences over to the world.

My memories of that day and the days leading up to it are as sharp as a knife's edge; but even if they weren't, I would discover that there are interesting ways of double-checking my recollection. I feel the events of that time as if they are happening now. And I suppose in a sense they are, alive in every street, in every American face you see, young or old. As a result, this book is not a backward glance at history. I want to take you on a journey to experience the "Dream" as it happened to me—and as I helped make it happen. You are holding an exploration of how an indelible moment is cobbled together, of what happened and how that shapes today and the days to come. It is the anatomy of an accident—or, at least, what I might have taken as accidental if I believed moments like these could ever have their roots in caprice. Martin often paraphrased Victor Hugo's *History of a Crime,* reminding those of us who worked with him that "nothing is more powerful than an idea whose time has come." Where the idea has come *from,* well, that's another story.

The March on Washington for Jobs and Freedom has been called an ocean of humanity. Maybe that is so. I know this: Where there is an ocean, there is a tide. And Wednesday, August 28, 1963, was the day the tide turned.

Clarence B. Jones
and Stuart Connelly
August 2010
Palo Alto, California

CHAPTER ONE

HISTORY IN
THE MAKING

The author with Dr. King at a press conference announcing the settlement agreement with the City of Birmingham ending segregation of downtown department stores, lunch counters, and public facilities.

Photo: Ernst Haas/Getty Images

They cried, and their cry came up unto God by reason of their bondage.

—Exodus 2:23

RANDOLPH'S LEGACY

Considering its colossal historic significance, there is a fundamental irony surrounding the 1963 March on Washington: It was not actually the brainchild of the Civil Rights Movement, nor even an idea borne of the 1960s.

More than a generation earlier, in 1941, the president of the Brotherhood of Sleeping Car Porters, A. Philip Randolph, had conceived of the original "March on Washington" as a way to pressure President Franklin D. Roosevelt into ensuring Negroes had jobs in the bustling American industries jump-started by our nation's entrance into World War II. Among historians he is widely acknowledged as the ideological godfather of our August 28, 1963 "March on Washington for Jobs and Freedom." Randolph's proposed demonstration was a serious, organized affair, and in fact the looming shadow of the event was enough pressure for Roosevelt. He was able to negotiate the march's cancellation with Randolph at the last minute only by giving in. Roosevelt issued the country's first Presidential Executive Order protecting African American rights in the twentieth century. It was only the second such order in our country's history (the first had been the Emancipation Proclamation), and the long time between these two presidential orders had not been kind to African Americans. Randolph moved on to other tactics—in 1948 his Committee Against Jim Crow in Military Service was instrumental in guiding President Harry S. Truman to issue his own decree (Executive Order 9981) banning racial discrimination in the military—but deep down he saw the rally as a missed opportunity.

Twenty-one years after his canceled march, Randolph was very carefully following the unsuccessful campaign of Martin Luther King, Jr. to desegregate public accommodations and facilities in Albany, Georgia. Bayard Rustin was one of Martin's close advisors and had been mentored by Randolph years earlier. In the late spring of 1963, Randolph reached out to Bayard and talked to him about the possibility of staging a large demonstration in Washington, D.C. as a retooled version of his idea. It was a notion that he had never relinquished. Trying ideas out on each other, Bayard and Randolph eventually envisioned a two-day program of organized rallies, linking civil rights to the national economic demands of working-class people. They planned to put together a coalition to bring in labor unions and unorganized workers in protest. They imagined sit-ins at congressional offices and similar "direct-action" strategies that would force lawmakers to take notice. Excited, Bayard agreed to suggest the concept to the Southern Christian Leadership Conference (SCLC), Dr. King's civil rights organization of black clergymen. Martin had formalized the SCLC in early 1957 following the yearlong 1956 bus boycott in Montgomery, Alabama that he had spearheaded. With the success of that boycott, he saw the power a tight affiliation of religious leaders could bring to a problem and understood that the way to make further progress was to become further organized.

Bayard came to Martin at a fortunate point in time. After the successful campaign that led to the desegregation of public facilities and department stores in Birmingham, Alabama in May 1963, Martin and other civil rights leaders began informal discussions to consider their next strategic move. Across the country Martin had many friends among the clergy as well as laypeople, but at that time the two people he consulted with almost daily were New Yorkers: Stanley Levison and me. We were among his closest advisors on matters of fund raising, political strategy, and how to deal most effectively with the media.[1] So when Bayard presented Martin with The March as a potential opportunity, Stanley and I were part of the strategic brain trust that considered the pros and cons. Stanley was a smart and dedicated New York businessman. He was also Jewish and white. Bayard had introduced him to Martin in 1956. Stanley became devoted to Martin and remained a tireless supporter of The Movement and the King legacy until his death in 1979. Stanley was a well-educated lawyer who had plenty of other options to pursue in his life; I have always considered that his work in support of Dr. King made him worthy of our nation's highest civilian award for outstanding public service.

Together, along with Martin's other advisors—Harry Wachtel, Cleveland Robinson, Professor Lawrence Reddick, and Reverends Thomas Kilgore, Walter Fauntroy, Wyatt Tee Walker, Andy Young, and Ralph Abernathy—we formed Dr.

King's inner circle. Unknown to us at the time, the FBI turned out to be a silent partner in that inner circle as well.

My home and office phones were tapped by the federal government. They had been watching me on and off for more than five years, and it would continue for another four. I wouldn't see actual evidence of this surveillance for almost twenty years, but it didn't surprise me when I learned of its existence. Martin always thought my caution bordered on paranoia, but during my time in the military I had had some experience with the people who make the rules, and I knew they did not play by them. And though the wiretaps may have been illegal, I can imagine that permission to set them was not hard to obtain, the times being what they were. We were square in the middle of the deepest part of the Cold War, and if any government organization, particularly an investigatory agency like the FBI, slapped a communist label on you, regardless of the facts, all the rules went out the window. Whether his suspicions were right or wrong, when FBI Director J. Edgar Hoover decided to play the "red" card with anyone, the Justice Department would approve the surveillance request. And with the stroke of Attorney General Robert Kennedy's pen, the Civil Rights Movement leaders' right to privacy was merely another casualty in the war against the Soviet Union. The methodology is not too far off from the post–September 11, 2001 hysteria; some inverted version of the PATRIOT Act that said America must invade the privacy of men and women peacefully striving to achieve freedom and equality for all. It was as if spying on citizens is clearly underscored in our Declaration of Independence or our national anthem, anywhere we crow to the world about how open and compassionate we are as a nation.

Well, Martin Luther King, Jr., Bayard Rustin, Stanley Levison, and I had nothing to hide. At first, anyway. That would soon change. Before the month of June was out we would be in the position of trying to obfuscate Stanley and Martin's working relationship and believing we were getting away with it. But for the time being, had we known we were wiretapped, it wouldn't have changed the substance of the conversations one bit.

There was, in retrospect, some upside to the invasion of privacy. Part of our strategy was to make the government nervous, and it happened effortlessly. As we talked about the logistics of such an undertaking, the government listened. As we moved closer to an understanding of just what needed to be done, they worried. And when we came up with a plan to stage The March effectively, the government shuddered at what it could mean for race relations in America. Because, regardless of whether it is just or not, any ruling body depends on the stability of the status quo. In that era, Negroes were second-class citizens, and the machinery of society seemed to hum along just fine under that pretense. Equality may well be good for black people, but no one was sure what a level racial playing field would mean to the nation as a whole. Segregation may have been hellish, but it was the devil we all knew.

We understood that if those in authority learned about our idea for a demonstration, it might well be regarded as a threat to the stability of our government. What we didn't know was that our plans were already being broadcast to the highest levels of government. During the early summer days of 1963, hundreds upon hundreds of transcript pages were piling up concerning the conversations we were having about The March:

Martin Luther King, Jr., had also been thinking about some new and larger form of demonstration. He said to his aides, "We are on a breakthrough. . . . We need a mass protest," and told them that offers of help had come from certain trade unions and from Paul Newman and Marlon Brando—both "Kennedy men."[2]

***

King asked the aides to contact Randolph to see if they could all work together.

***

Jones called an unwoman [unknown woman] and told her that Dr. Martin L. King was coming to town today, and would be staying at his house.

***

Reverend King stated that he planned to attend a conference soon with leaders of other organizations in order to discuss the March on Washing-

ton with them. Levison suggested to King that
King take advantage of the two public appearances
he will make in New York City, during the coming
week, to announce his plans for the March on
Washington and the demonstrations that will go
along with it.

Yes, the government had a direct line to all our planning and strategy. The question that information brought to the door of the Kennedy White House was: What, if anything, was the government going to do about it?

HOME AWAY FROM HOME

The FBI had some understanding of what was at stake for American Negroes. For example, I find the subtext in this declassified FBI summary memo illuminating:

On June 11th—the same day that Kennedy made his
historic civil rights speech and the eve of Medgar
Evers's murder—King announced to the press plans
for a march on Washington.

Now, domestic intelligence write-ups are not typically valued for their editorial content, but this memo tied together both the hopeful—Kennedy's speech—and the dreadful—Evers' horrible slaying—when it simply could have stated, "King announced plans for a march on Washington."[3] Why? Because everyone knew, even if they didn't all want to face it, that lives were on the line in the effort to remake America. That truth had a way of working its way out, seeping into the very air around us and creeping into minds of even the FBI agents who actually were *tasked* with preventing racial justice.

The March was happening. On July 2, less than a month after Martin's announcement, he and Randolph booked a conference room at the Roosevelt Hotel in midtown Manhattan. We held a meeting that was attended by nearly two dozen desegregation activists, including the other four Civil Rights Movement leaders who, along with Martin and Randolph, comprised the "Big Six": John Lewis, Roy Wilkins, James Farmer, and Whitney Young, Jr. It was in that room that The March organization was established. A vote was held to determine who would take on the vital role of chief coordinator. Bayard Rustin, one of The March's principal organizers, wanted the job. Unfortunately, he was met by opposition from some of the other leaders. There was Bayard's earlier membership in the Young Communist League to consider, some argued. A bigger stumbling block was his homosexuality. Even those closest to Bayard had to acknowledge that his 1953 conviction on morals charges could cause some problems. Bayard's reaction was that most people who *knew* him were aware of the conviction and that it was "old hat." Martin, referencing the Bible's Gospel of John (8:7), said something to the effect of "Let he who has not sinned cast the first stone." And when the vote was taken, Bayard was named chief coordinator. I loved him all the more for not backing down in the face of such harsh but, at the time, practical considerations.

There was little time to lose; with the crowded calendars of so many busy individuals to take into account, the August 28 date had not been chosen as much as backed into. If it wasn't going to happen then, it would have to wait until the following spring, something no one wanted. Bayard went into high gear in Randolph's Brotherhood of Sleeping Car Porters West 130th Street office, now the New York City headquarters of The March. He worked tirelessly there. Never mind the planning, in a matter of days he had written (and, with respect to the maps and charts, somewhat crudely illustrated) *Organizing Manual No. 1,* which would become the bible of The March. By mid-July Bayard had printed and distributed two thousand copies to Movement leaders all across the country in an effort to create a coordinated system that would allow us to pull off the demonstration on an extremely short timetable.

Martin had been of two minds regarding the entire enterprise. He knew that The March was the right idea and that Randolph's concept had come back around at just the right time. But Birmingham had taken a lot out of him. In the aftermath, he had wanted nothing more than to take his wife, Coretta, and his four children away for a vacation and forget—forget the looming deadline for his book (*Why We Can't*

Wait, Harper & Row, 1964), the office politics of running the ever-growing SCLC, the constant need to raise funds to sustain the staff and support the various civil rights programs, and the demands for appearances from all over the country that he had a difficult time turning down.

Martin had gone on record with his advisors, saying that he didn't believe he could plan such a massive undertaking under his usual working conditions, which consisted mainly of endless interruptions and demands for him to make decisions on projects outside the scope of what he was trying to accomplish at the time. No, if this march were going to come together under such a tight deadline (particularly with the issues of raising money and getting cooperation from other civil rights groups still up in the air), he would have to escape all the distractions. Get away to a place where very few people knew how to reach him.

The logistics of planning for the March on Washington dictated that Martin be available by phone and possibly in person while he was on "vacation," so he, Stanley, and I decided it made practical sense for him to stay at my home. Of course, what seemed a perfectly reasonable strategic move for Dr. King's leadership team was more like a headache for my wife, Anne, and our family—mostly because it required that we move out.

My family and I had returned to New York from Southern California in 1961 and settled in Riverdale, a suburban community in the West Bronx. At the time, our choice of location was influenced by the availability of good schools, public and private, and proximity to the residence of Arthur Kinoy, Esq., one of my legal mentors. Anne and I had rented a five-bedroom house while we awaited the construction of our new home on land we had purchased nearby. The spacious rental house was off 254th Street, next door to the Arturo Toscanini estate, and was a quick four-block walk from the Metro North Railroad station that headed into Grand Central Station. The house had an enormous sunken living room and a recreation room, but as we packed up to make the place ready for Martin and his family, I realized quickly what I would be missing most there at the beginning of a hot August: The deck overlooking the Hudson River and the nearby community pool to which we were about to turn over our access.

To compound matters, Anne and I were asked by Ralph Abernathy to find a rental home in Riverdale for him and his wife, Juanita. (Reverend Abernathy traveled with Dr. King on most civil rights demonstrations and considered himself a "co-leader" of the SCLC.) We had our hands full finding a place for ourselves. Anne and I eventually contacted neighbors we were friendly with, Peter and Cora Weiss, who generously allowed us to stay in their home for three weeks while they were vacationing in Martha's Vineyard, Massachusetts. This act of unselfish generosity by the Weisses in support of Martin was singularly important to the strategic planning of the March on Washington. Anne felt especially put upon because she was the one to follow up on all the calls I made to neighbors trying to enlist their assistance in finding a house for the Abernathys.

But for all this clumsy shuffling around, we worked quietly. The plan was that no one from the outside world should be able to penetrate Martin's getaway, and we managed to pull that off—sort of. According to a memo from the Atlanta field office of the FBI to J. Edgar Hoover:

```
Jones states that only four individuals will know
where King will be staying.
```

Yes, four individuals and the entire Justice Department.

While Martin was there, my house was the de facto command and control center for the SCLC. Away from the hectic day-to-day activity in Atlanta, he was able to fully concentrate on the work at hand. During the weekends, Anne would go with our children to her mother's house in Wilton, Connecticut. I would remain in Riverdale so I could be available to Martin, and Stanley would consult with me by phone. Together, the three of us started to sort out how the mechanics of The March might work. It was a logistical operation on a scale we had never attempted. The churches, which always played a pivotal role, were absolutely critical here. They were the way to focus the "ground troops"—those people who wanted to change the world but didn't feel empowered to take an individual public stand. Naturally, there was an enormous difference between a focused and goal-oriented endeavor like a local bus boycott and a massive drive across the country to illustrate an overarching point about segregation and racial inequality. Travel operations were going to play a major role. People might be willing to march from the Washington Monument to our planned destination, the Capitol steps, but someone had to get them to the Washington Monument first.

Meanwhile, as we were laying out the blueprint of how to bring the masses into the nation's capital in a show of faith, hope, and solidarity, those in power continued to listen and were also considering their options very, very carefully.

SPIN BEFORE THERE WAS SPIN

Nowadays most people know all about the concept of political "spin." But in 1963 there was no pocket-sized word for it. Still, methods of attempting to control events by controlling perception have existed at least since Machiavelli, and there were many people on Capitol Hill who knew how to deploy those methods with vicious efficiency. Why, this attempt at control is very nearly the entire founding charter of the Central Intelligence Agency.

There were so many parties interested in a preemptive downplaying of The March's potential for success that it sometimes seemed we were wildly outnumbered. The Civil Rights Movement was at war with the status quo; we had always known that. And we knew it had always been a war of public opinion. But The March was different—if those in power had their way, the battle over the nation's perception of it would be a cold war, a clandestine war if at all possible. It was a clash whose winner, it struck me, would be decided before the first performer appeared in the dawn light on the Washington Mall.

The history books may tell us John F. Kennedy supported the March on Washington, but the truth is a bit murkier. In fact, the president's initial strategy was simply to try to persuade the leadership to cancel The March. In the summer of 1963, President Kennedy's Civil Rights Bill was in play in the House of Representatives. It amounted to his stance on the issue of America's Negro population, his choice for the nation's policy of tolerance, and his administration was not in the market for other ideas on the subject. "We want success in Congress, not just a big show at the Capitol" was the president's message. "Some of these people are looking for an excuse to be against us and I don't want to give any of them a chance to say 'Yes, I'm for the bill, but I am damned if I will vote for it at the point of a gun.'"[4]

Kennedy's arguments fell on deaf ears, of course. And political animal that he was, after he realized there was no way for him to prevent The March, he took the next logical step: He got on the bandwagon. This bit of political footwork would go a long way to cementing his family's image as fighters for the downtrodden.

But behind the scenes, the attorney general's enforcer—J. Edgar Hoover—continued to try to thwart our attempts at putting a cohesive demonstration together. As we approached the date of The March, the FBI turned up the previously smoldering heat on Hoover's campaign to bring Martin down to full rolling boil. It was character assassination, pure and simple. And un-American, one would like to think.[5] Among other tactics, Hoover tried to leverage information about Martin's sexual dalliances against The March, even though none of his supposed personal weaknesses had anything to do with The Movement as a whole.[6]

For the time being, the weapon of choice for people within and outside of the government who opposed The March was a time-honored method in Washington: Spreading untraceable information. The off-the-record quote. The press leak. The whisper campaign. As we had expected, Bayard's homosexuality, prior criminal convictions, and socialist leanings were first out of the gate. Our organization took a few knocks, but it all blew over quickly and was nothing that could derail The March.

Those who opposed us were desperate to find that leverage point that would deflate the number of marchers. If they could cut our numbers down, the effect would be devastating. If supporter turnout appeared anemic, everything in the media coverage (and hence the general world opinion) would focus on our disappointment and paint a picture of The March as a failure.

But the flip side of that strategy existed too. If enough people turned out, the world press would say we had brought the government to its knees. The media, as I am not the first person to point out, works on the poles of the human experience, not the middle ground.

So success in Washington would be all about perception. If, in the weeks leading up to The March, it seemed that it was going to be a washout, people would not come, and it would indeed become a washout. When you get into the basic mechanics of it, action is based on decision—should I or shouldn't I?—and all manner of conscious and subliminal cues attend that decision: Second guessing, flip-flopping, fear. Something takes off like a rocket only when it seems inevitable. A marketer's job is to take all that doubt away so that whatever he's hawking feels very much like a fait accompli. *It's a best-seller, everyone's reading it. Eventually you'll read it, might as well buy it now.* Our march needed to do that too. But it was less like an advertising campaign than a political campaign, because we had an opponent just as dedicated to the opposite result. Both tactics were valid: No one wants to be the only guest to a party, and no one wants to miss the party everyone's going to be talking about. History would judge who had the better PR effort.

The March had coordinating offices in many of the major cities along the eastern seaboard as well as in Chicago, Detroit,

Birmingham, and Los Angeles. Ted Brown, one of Randolph's organizers out of the March Committee's Washington, D.C. office, called Martin at my house on August 10. He reported that Washington was "running from fear, everybody's scared stiff around here. Leaves have been cancelled for hospital personnel, police and all long distance telephone operators."

This gave us a nice boost of confidence. Ted went on to say that Burke Marshall, Robert Kennedy's deputy attorney general on civil rights, was terrified as well. "They are all afraid in Washington because of the possibility of violence," he reported with a certain amount of glee. According to Ted, the District of Columbia's chief of police, Robert V. Murray, had put the entire department on the highest level of alert. Officers were scheduled for eighteen-hour shifts instead of the typical eight hours.

That fear in the nation's capital that Ted referenced was also reflected in the attitude and state of mind of many political leaders and some in the media at the time.[7] Jack Eisen, one of the columnists for *The Washington Post,* wrote several pieces that raised all sorts of dire possibilities and predictions of violence and disorder that would likely take place if The March occurred. In an August 18 article he rhetorically asked, "Will Washington Negroes accept the leadership that has brought them this far or will they turn to the extremists? Will future historians record that Washington made a successful transition with peace and pride, or will they record a failure that was marked by turmoil and violence?"[8]

Covering its bases, the opposition, which consisted of some highly conservative black clergy as well as white people from the South and elsewhere who were not in support of Dr. King and the Civil Rights Movement, fanned the flames in both directions of the racial divide, a well-worn but always useful political tactic. Even if we Negroes were peaceable, went the argument, what about those virulent racists who would come looking to exact revenge for our audacity with clubs and knives? Martin believed that the people who raised the issue of possible violence and disorder during or from The March most fervently were simply opposed to our show of solidarity and viewed this scare tactic as the best way to stop it. He addressed this point with his customary dry sense of humor one evening as we were working in Riverdale, wondering aloud, "Why would people travel all that distance to a peaceful demonstration for the principal purpose of engaging in violence and disorder? It seems like a long way to go."

Indeed it did.

One of the early issues fueling the fear and possible disorder in the minds of those in power was our initial plan of having the marchers assemble on the steps of the U.S. Capitol Building. The Kennedy Administration came out against this idea—strongly against it. But we were determined that Martin Luther King would speak from the very top step.

Nothing would dissuade us.

DIVIDED WE STOOD

Although in 1963 Martin Luther King and his SCLC commanded national attention in a way no other civil rights group did, the organization had no intention of tackling the massive undertaking of The March alone. Both the ideology of The Movement and the logistics of The March dictated that, in order for the event to succeed, it would have to be a team effort. CORE (the Congress of Racial Equality), the NAACP (the National Association for the Advancement of Colored People), NUL (the National Urban League), SNCC (the Student Nonviolent Coordinating Committee), NCNW (the National Council of Negro Women), and labor unions under the leadership of A. Philip Randolph and Walter Reuther (of the United Auto Workers) all had skin in this particular game.

The trick was to balance all of the various agendas. We were working side by side with many noble-minded groups, and though in general one could say they all had the same vision for improving the Negroes' condition in America, it was actually more complicated than that. Each organization had similar goals but different strategies for achieving those goals. As different as each of the groups' leaders were, it is hardly surprising that every organization looked at the struggle of blacks through slightly different eyes. And this led to very different views on The March itself.

Roy Wilkins, the national executive secretary of the NAACP, for example, wanted to focus The March almost exclusively on legislative reform. That mirrored his (and his constituents') belief that working the legal angle was the key to racial equality. There were those within the March's Organizing Committee who saw the event as a rallying cry in support of the passage of Kennedy's Civil Rights Bill. Yet there were some who saw the Civil Rights Bill as watered down and ineffectual. Others viewed our demonstration as a condemnation of the Kennedy Administration, a way of sending a message of our disenchantment and frustration with the White House's "foot-dragging" on getting a true civil rights bill passed into law.

There were interests outside of the legislation as well. Some factions were more concerned with issues of poverty among blacks. Some contingents of The Movement supported The March primarily as a vehicle to focus the nation's attention on overcoming educational barriers.[9] And, of course, there were members of the March Committee who, along with their supporters, saw the demonstration as focusing principally on the need for better jobs and improved working conditions for blacks.

John Lewis, the chairman of SNCC, wanted to stir the Negroes themselves to immediate action, while others wanted to thrust the burden of change into the laps of those in power. Each participating organization had its own take on which direction to set the public posture and perception of The March.

Against this background, Martin and those of us who represented him were confronted with the exact same office politics he found throughout Atlanta's SCLC headquarters—the same politics he had been trying to escape by using my home as a refuge. The distractions had followed him to New York and taken root in The March planning. Along with the growing sense of importance The March acquired came, apparently, a requisite amount of squabbling. What became clear very quickly in those early weeks of August was that we had a lot of generals and very few foot soldiers. Among the more contentious issues in our preparation was the order of speakers from the various groups comprising the umbrella organizations of The March and how much time would be allotted for each one to speak. This powder keg involved not only the obvious issue of time constraints but also the delicate maneuvering among a minefield of egos. Now, I'm the first to admit that Martin King had an ego. But I can also say that in this case, the man truly let the circumstances before him pave the way for his response, while many of the other organizers seemed at least as concerned with how they were perceived personally as with how The March as a whole worked. We were blessed to have the overarching wisdom and guidance of A. Philip Randolph to act as a steady compass pointing the way in a stormy sea of egos.

Nowhere was this clash of personalities easier to see than in the discussions about the speaker schedule. People were pushing for a uniform time limit of five minutes for every speech. Martin did not agree with that, but felt he should not personally object, concerned that it might inflame petty jealousies among his brethren. The sad truth is that, human nature being what it is, there *was* some jealousy of Martin's national stature among the civil rights leadership. It was not hard for people toiling in The Movement to watch Martin's rise to prominence and say to themselves, Why isn't that me? I understand that instinct. However, that doesn't make it right. Under such circumstances, Stanley, Bayard, Martin, and I, in all of our "sidebar" telephone conversations or in-person meetings, concluded that it would be inappropriate for it to appear as if Martin were pushing himself to be the speaker with the most time allotted. Yet time restraints remained an issue of principal concern to all of us throughout August. Martin felt there were too many speakers and that the time reserved for him was not sufficient. Because of this, he wondered aloud if "they are trying to throttle me. Maybe they're determined that I not be in a position of making a speech that will get a great response from the people." Now, this may sound like an egotistical man, but from everything we had been hearing, a significant percentage of the potential crowd was coming to Washington specifically to hear Martin Luther King, Jr. speak. We had to make a tough call: Is it better to placate other leaders of the Civil Rights Movement or to give the crowd what it was expecting?

Where did I come down on that? The FBI knew:

> On August 21, 1963, a confidential source, who has
> furnished reliable information in the past, ad-
> vised that on that date, CLARENCE JONES held a
> discussion with an unidentified individual re-
> garding the March on Washington. According to
> this source . . . JONES indicated that he was un-
> happy about the time limitation which had been
> placed on the March on Washington speakers, lim-
> iting everyone alike to five minutes. JONES states
> that his proposal was that Dr. King be introduced
> by Randoph [*sic*], that he be the last speaker and
> be allotted the most time to speak.

It fell upon me to have some frank conversations. I talked the situation over with Cleveland Robinson. Affectionately known as Cleve, he was an international vice president of the District 65 Retail Wholesale Workers Union, whose headquarters at the time was located on the Lower East Side in Manhattan. District 65 was one of the most consistent sources of financial support and foot soldiers to Martin and his SCLC. Six foot four and partially blind, Cleve had a booming baritone voice tinged with a Jamaican accent and a take-no-prisoners attitude you could see in his face. Together Cleve, Stanley, and I came up with a game plan.

It was simple: We had to make sure that the people who were universally supported by the committee members were on our side. Bayard, the chief coordinator, was well respected for his organizational leadership abilities, but he wasn't enough. We knew just from the pushback during the original vote for that position that people were not going to hold their tongues if they disagreed with Bayard. Members of the organizing committee may have been convinced to let go of their concern about his past "communist leaning" or his prior arrest and conviction for homosexual conduct. But, on an issue such as the order of speakers and the time allotted to each one, they would stand their ground. No, Cleve and I knew the silver bullet in all this was A. Philip Randolph. The man understood politics. This was someone whom I had heard say on several occasions, "Nothing counts but pressure, pressure, more pressure." He was the revered elder statesman of The March. We knew if he agreed that Martin should be the de facto keynote speaker, it would be so. This would be in keeping with what we believed was the overwhelming sentiment of the people coming to The March.

I presented our case to Bayard and Randolph, insisting that it was the right thing for The March (not for Martin, mind you, but for *The March*) that Martin be the last and longest speaker. They agreed with my reasoning. It was then decided that either Cleve or I would be the "heavies" in conversations with the other leaders—Roy Wilkins (NAACP), Jim Farmer (CORE), Whitney Young (NUL), and the other march organizers to explain our position.

As Martin's lawyer and political advisor, I was used to tough negotiating on his behalf. Several of The March leaders, however, had never seen me in this role, up close and personal. I honestly didn't mind, nor was I reluctant to be the guy putting his foot down. And I wasn't shy about pulling out my ace in the hole, a line that never failed to ruffle feathers: "Believe me, my brothers, nobody here will want to follow Martin as a public speaker."

How true that turned out to be.

In the end, the other organizers agreed to our plan and, in doing so, paved the way for a chapter of American history that helped shape the nation as we know it today. At the time, however, it didn't look like things were going to go that way. The mood in the room was more one of resentment and capitulation than of understanding that we were marching into the dawn of a new era. But isn't that always the way with history? You are so busy worrying about the minor details that you're unaware that the world is on the verge of true change.

PLAGUED BY DOUBT

The continuing pressure of the deadline compounded all our differences of opinion. Everyone was irritable; each one thought he was right. An endless stream of reports was pouring into my Riverdale home (now converted into what we called Martin's "command post north"). Everyone was working overtime to bring the event together, and the phone was ringing off the hook with updates from the field. Unfortunately, every bit of good news was canceled out by some nugget of worrisome information.

Ted Brown called again, this time to fill us in on attendance projections. He told Martin that the best-guess estimate was 150,000 people, which was not bad, but it was not the stellar number we were hoping for either. Ted said he was quite worried about support for The March from residents in the D.C. area: "I don't think we will get as much as five thousand Negroes out of Washington."

To me, it was nothing short of bizarre to think that blacks coming from as far away as California would be spending days to get to The March while a large percentage of those who were having the party thrown in their backyard might not bother to attend.

Ted's answer was a simple one: "Not too many Negro ministers are involved from here."

It wasn't a publicity or public relations misstep; it was more straightforward than that. People do what their leaders ask them to do. We would need to make a fast, concerted effort to get those in charge of Washington's black churches on track with the demonstration.

Ted also shared his concern about the distance of The March locale to the majority of SCLC's constituency— people living in Alabama, Georgia, Mississippi, and the rest of the southern states. He suggested that the only way to get a significant number of attendees from the South was to rent trains. We weren't even sure that this was possible, but the suggestion went on our list just the same. At this point, almost no ideas were too far afield for the coordinating committee to consider.[10]

Steven Courier, a respected and influential New York philanthropist, had pledged a contribution to The March of fifty-one chartered buses to help with the estimated thirty thousand people who would be coming to Washington from New York City. And we were able to charter three private planes coming out of California in addition to the plane we had already chartered to carry a hand-picked group of entertainers. It was a start, but the transportation issue continued to frustrate us.

There was, however, some good news. We heard that the participation out of Detroit should be high, primarily because of the United Auto Workers' association with The Movement. The Protestant and Catholic churches were going all out to try to get their members to attend. In fact, even though school was not in session, Catholic churches in Washington made an effort to encourage all their parochial students to join The March.

Still, A. Philip Randolph continued to be concerned with the apparent overall lack of interest among Negroes in Washington. *The Afro-American,* a leading black newspaper in the D.C. area, printed a letter to the editor suggesting that there was general apathy toward The March among Northern blacks.[11]

It was a refrain we heard again and again. Reverend Thomas Kilgore, a close friend of Martin's and then pastor of the Friendship Baptist Church in Harlem, told him in a mid-August phone call, "It looks like there may be more white people than Negroes."

This really upset Martin. "We can't afford to have fewer than 100,000 people and there has to be more Negroes than Whites," he replied. This was always a tough issue to navigate. We all knew that Negroes needed to be seen as handling their affairs themselves. And yet part of the struggle was to show the white world that there were plenty of white people who did not engage in racism, who supported our struggle for equal treatment, who condemned segregation. In fact, one of the key reasons Malcolm X and some other militant community leaders decried The March was because it wasn't planned as a black-only show of strength.

Tom maintained he was trying to get 150,000 people to The March from around the country. Though not as big a number as we wanted, I nevertheless couldn't help wondering how serious it would look in a long television shot; the entire Washington Mall packed with our people.

Martin asked Tom's opinion of the Washington-area clergy's responsibility in pulling together a big crowd. Both men agreed that they had to contact ministers in the area in an effort to encourage them to boost march support in those final days.

Tom told Martin that after he preached Sunday morning, he was going to Washington. "We're going to put six men in Washington and Baltimore," he said, meaning members of the March Committee assigned to drum up participation from those communities. "We already have three guys in Philadelphia and they've estimated there will be fifteen thousand coming from there."

As if in an effort to assuage our nerves, Tom piled on other reports that painted a somewhat better picture. There were at least seven buses coming from Norfolk, Virginia. Martin's brother Alfred (A.D. to those close to him) was working to charter a train for a thousand people out of Birmingham. We contemplated trying to book twelve trains to carry a thousand marchers each directly from New York City and sixty buses that could come out of Long Island carrying another three thousand people.

"The whole Eastern Seaboard is aflame with this," Tom told Martin. "You can't find a bus to rent in New York now." He gave Martin an estimate of thirty-five thousand people coming from New York, then suggested that might be a conservative number.

The phone call ended on a foreboding note. Tom asked if we should consider stopping marchers who were arriving in their cars on the outskirts of town, having them park, and shuttling them in to avoid horrific gridlock.

Martin thought for a moment. Then he responded, his low voice caught for eternity, snagged in the FBI wiretap dragnet: "Tom, I don't think they ought to block people from driving into Washington. If it's necessary to paralyze the city for the whole day, then it's necessary."

THE CELEBRITY DELEGATION

We had The March budgeted at a staggering $120,000, which is the equivalent of nearly $1 million in today's dollars. But we didn't *have* that money. We received large, generous financial gifts from many people of means, unsung Americans who wanted to do what was right. We couldn't have attempted The March without that support. But we also had to find a way to pass the hat to the general public. And the key to that was offering affordable, easily carried mementos. One could get an official March on Washington lapel pin for only twenty-five cents, and nearly two hundred thousand were sold with a week still to go before the March even took place. It's hard to say how much they cost to manufacture, but I know they were each a tiny little tin piece of profit. It all went back into The March organization coffers.

The official March souvenirs were a series of five small posters designed by Louis Lo Monaco. They were rendered in the flag colors red, white, and blue with black and white photographs. Lo Monaco used both hopeful and painful Movement iconography: One poster featured a police dog attack, but the next, a human chain of hand holding. The phrase "We Shall Overcome" appeared ripped from somewhere else and recklessly glued into place, a twenty-year precursor to punk rock album art. With the posters, we sought to depict the unique significance of the event. The organizers believed that the artwork for each poster transmitted their sense of hope and urgency to all those who may have been undecided in attending. Forty thousand of each version were printed and sold in advance for a dollar each. The beauty of this approach as a fund-raiser was that, although supporters could choose to buy single posters, the sense that the whole, unified portfolio was greater than the sum of its parts steered people toward ordering all five. The finances were coming together, and in addition to raising capital for The March organizers, these pre-sold items gave us something perhaps even more valuable than money: They gave us a sense that the zeitgeist was on our side. We did whatever we could to raise The March's profile and encouraged others to do the same.

For example, shortly before the end of August, writer James Baldwin, singer Josephine Baker, and actor Burt Lancaster held their own small march along the streets of Paris to call attention to ours. The press in France—a country that has always taken great interest in America's racial problems—reacted enthusiastically, and it wouldn't surprise me if some French citizens made arrangements to attend after seeing or reading about their own small Parisian version.

As the date of the March on Washington approached, I began turning more of my attention to coordinating with entertainer and activist Harry Belafonte on the logistics of arrival and participation of the so-called celebrity delegation.

Martin was not particularly enamored with the Hollywood lifestyle of consumption and superficiality, but he was a realist. The power of the celebrity contingent was quite simply to attract eyeballs; they knew it and we knew it. Actors and musicians could (and still do) capture the attention of what might potentially be an otherwise inattentive or distracted television audience. While we were concerned about the number of people physically at The March, we were even more worried about how our march's energy would translate to a TV audience. You have to be riveting or risk being tuned out. We reasoned that the presence of Hollywood celebrities would be a strong TV audience driver.

The irony was that Martin had slowly but surely been building up his own form of international celebrity. He found that slightly embarrassing, but he was not above using it to The Movement's advantage. In fact, his star power was, in our estimation, what would finally drive the attendance of our march to where we needed it to be. It was why we insisted Martin have the position of last speaker. That, my friends, is show business.

And so, just as The March needed Martin, Martin needed the celebrities. Luckily, despite the narcissistic tendencies of some in the entertainment business, many stars either have or need to believe they have wide-open hearts and gravitate toward liberal-leaning politics. Either way, they could help us, and we were taking them up on their offer.

Harry Belafonte, artist that he is, preferred to think of the group as the "cultural" delegation. During the two to three weeks in August 1963 preceding The March, he went throughout Los Angeles rattling cages in film studio suites and recording studio booths to try to get the hottest talent in America to participate. He advised me that the "chairman" of the delegation, Charlton Heston, would be arriving by private charter plane from Los Angeles with the other participants. Among the celebrities who would be traveling with him were Marlon Brando, Shelley Winters, Steve McQueen, James Garner, Tony Franciosa, Judy Balaban, Sidney Poitier, Sammy Davis, Jr., Diahann Carroll, Paul Newman and his wife, Joanne Woodward, and, fresh from their march in France, Burt Lancaster and Josephine Baker.

In August 1963, these celebrities were at the height of their popularity, and their attitudes and opinions carried real weight in America. But just what would they do to improve race relations? They would wave, they would pose for pictures. They would grant interviews to select media outlets and go over our talking points. Some would perform, and some would even speak at the podium. In general, they would mingle and create a surging sense of importance on top of the already intense philosophical issues we had brought to the foreground.

Although it was not as difficult then as it is these days, getting in touch with celebrities, wrangling them, and pinning them down to a particular day and date was not so easy a task. At Harry's direction, I spent endless mornings rushing into Manhattan meetings with New York–based agents or the occasional star him- or herself. Afternoons I kept busy calling talent agencies on the West Coast from my temporary home. In the end, the celebrities responded en masse to Harry Belafonte's appeal for them to join him in The March and try to change America. That was too juicy a role for them to turn down. It was also a testament to Harry's stature in the entertainment industry and the industry's acknowledgment of just how close he had become to Martin Luther King, Jr. since their initial meeting during the Montgomery Bus Boycott in 1956.[12]

But it wasn't just Washington where celebrities were pitching in. On Friday, August 23, the Apollo Theatre had a March on Washington fund-raiser. Quincy Jones, Thelonious Monk, and Tony Bennett were just some of the acts that took the stage. I loved those artists, but I was unable to attend. The evening of that amazing concert, I still was far too busy with details.

Once the composition, transport, and arrival of the celebrity delegation fell into place, I was free to travel to Washington and catch up with the other organizers. It was now Monday, August 26, and time was becoming the enemy.

Anne wanted to join me on the trip. We discussed it at length, but I insisted I didn't have the time to be worrying about my wife and young children in the middle of this unknown and unknowable undertaking. Of course I wanted her there, but who knew for sure what would happen? Fights could break out on Constitution Avenue. National Guardsmen could start launching tear gas. A Ku Klux Klansman could start firing from the top of the Washington Monument. Perhaps the idea of an outbreak of violence at The March wasn't merely (or only) a public relations tool. It was likely my family would be safer remaining in New York.

Anne certainly deserved to be at The March in person. I wouldn't have been working with Martin if it had not been for her insistence that I meet with him when he first reached out to me. At the time, I was just starting to pursue a career in entertainment law; I was squeezing what I could out of the material world—new cars and custom-tailored suits— and enjoying it. Judge Hubert Delaney, a mentor of mine, called to say that this Reverend Martin Luther King, Jr., who had been making headlines recently, needed some pro bono help on a tax evasion charge in Alabama. I could not have cared less about the civil rights struggle in 1960. As I talked to Judge Delaney, who had recommended me to Martin, all I could think was, "Just because some Negro preacher got his hand caught in the cookie jar stealing, that is not my problem." (So much for innocent until proven guilty.)

Anne read me the riot act when I got off the phone. How could I say no to Martin Luther King, Jr.? Easy: "No."

But one thing about Martin, he didn't take no for an answer often. He showed up at my house in Altadena, California, to ask for my help in person. I was not the type to get star-struck easily, so I begged off, politely telling him that my career needed attention, I had bills, I had responsibilities. I had a family to support.

Although he respected my decision, Dr. King asked me to come see him preach as a guest pastor at a Baptist church in Baldwin Hills the coming Sunday. I said I wasn't much of a church-goer, but Martin had woven his spell on Anne, and with a little arm-twisting from her I eventually agreed to go. It would be a church service that changed the trajectory of my life from there on out.[13]

I had Anne to thank, so yes, perhaps we should have made arrangements for someone to look after the children and gone to The March together. But though my simple concerns for her safety were easy to underscore, that was not the entire breadth of my reasoning at the time. There was something else, something I kept to myself. A part of me needed to go off on this adventure alone for reasons I could not explain then. I loved my family very much, and these marchers for whom I was turning my back on Anne were strangers. But they needed salvation. I believed they needed my help and that there was something I could do for them. It never occurred to me that I might be depriving Anne and my children of the opportunity for their own salvation as well. The March wasn't only for the downtrodden and impoverished—it was a kind of baptism for everyone who attended. I decided it was better for Anne to remain behind and, because of that, she missed out on a defining moment. The decision lives on with me—a true regret.

Early on in the planning stages, I had hoped to take the train to D.C. with Stanley Levison. It wasn't in the cards for

us, sadly. Our march occurred too late for that. As I alluded
to earlier, a time came when we had to change Martin's working relationship with Stanley. Two months earlier, after that
June civil rights meeting with the president in the Cabinet
Room, Kennedy asked to take a walk with Martin in the
White House Rose Garden. There, JFK disclosed to Martin
a startling piece of intelligence: J. Edgar Hoover had told the
president that Stanley and Jack O'Dell were "communist
agents of Moscow."[14] Now Kennedy made it clear that the
Civil Rights Movement could not afford to have Martin
dragged down by a "Soviet conspiracy;" he "recommended"
that Martin sever all ties to Jack and Stanley. No less a figure
than the President of the United States was telling Martin
who his friends should be.

SECRET

Communist Party, United States of America (CPUSA)
Negro Question
Communist Influence on Racial Matters

A third confidential source, who
has furnished reliable information
in the past, advised in August, 1962,
that Stanley Levison is a secret member
of the CPUSA

(S)

Dealing with Jack O'Dell was not the big problem. Though he had been the director of the New York office of the SCLC and later one of its directors of voter registration, he was not as close to Martin as Stanley was. Even though he was quite skillful and as dedicated to our work as anyone, Jack simply was not nearly as *personally* valuable to Martin. The decision was made even easier by Jack himself, who, when we discussed the issue with him directly, fought back fiercely. He invoked the ideas of oppressive governments and free politics. As it turned out, he was correct in his political analysis of some of the possible consequences of, as he put it, "caving in to Hoover." But we were forced to make a strategic judgment about the consequences to Martin's leadership and influence with the government should his relationship with Jack continue. In the end, we let Jack go. I don't believe he ever forgave Martin or ever really understood the political leverage we would lose if we did not sever our organizational ties with him.

Stanley, upon hearing about the Rose Garden conversation from Martin the next day, did not make any fuss. In fact, he insisted that Martin immediately cease all *direct* contact with him. (I would become Martin's go-between, working on ideas and strategies with Stanley and then passing them along, so Martin could access Stanley's brilliance indirectly.)[15] Martin was loyal to Stanley, and I'm sure he would have stood by him if Stanley had even made the slightest argument, but Stanley was smart enough to see the big picture. He could see it was not a personal decision. Stanley's position was simple: Martin, his leadership, and The Movement were too important to have potential support from the Kennedy Administration compromised or undermined because of their relationship. That is one of the things that made him a great man. We jointly decided to terminate all direct contact between Martin and Stanley Levison. The man fell on his sword for the greater good of what he believed in. That was rare, even in the seemingly selfless world of the civil rights struggle. He was in the forefront of those many unsung heroes in our Movement.

Martin initially objected to this course of action, principally because of his great respect and affection for Stanley and, secondarily, because he knew that Stanley's "disassociation" from him, me, and the SCLC would deprive us of an invaluable asset. In addition, he bristled, as had Jack O'Dell, at the idea of the FBI and the government essentially telling us whom *they* regarded as "acceptable" for Martin's work and organization. That was downright un-American.

I agreed 100 percent with the validity of Martin's reasoning, but I also knew it didn't matter. Stanley Levison wouldn't risk coming back.

In discussing with Stanley whether he would attend The March, the issue was this: Would his presence with me around Martin provide Hoover and the FBI a basis to attack and discredit The March as "commie led" or "influenced?" Stanley was *not* a Soviet spy. But he had been a member of the Communist Party in his younger years, and that information had been uncovered by the FBI.

In the end we had to deprive Hoover of the opportunity to discredit us. Consequently, while I was in Washington, D.C., Stanley would be in New York, available to me by phone any time if I needed him, but not a participant. More like a ghost—another victim of that quiet war between the old ways and the coming new ways.

I boarded the train at Riverdale Station by myself. It was crammed with people heading to Grand Central Station, black faces and white alike. I wondered if some of these people would then switch trains with me to catch the D.C.-bound Afternoon Congressional. I wondered if some were heading to The March a bit early so they could settle in and catch their breath a little before things got swinging. I wondered if anybody besides the FBI and the Justice Department really cared at all.

NO TURNING BACK

As the train slowed alongside the platform in Washington, D.C.'s Union Station, conflicting emotions washed over me, a mingled sense of both anxiety and exhilaration. What we were planning to do in a few short days could be like the achievements we had accomplished in Birmingham multiplied by a factor of ten or more, in terms of its power (hence the exhilaration) but also in terms of the potential for police or agitator violence (hence the anxiety). It was a rush of a feeling, the sense of being on the edge of something vast.

As I gathered my valise and briefcase, I reflected on how many times I had had to leave Anne and our children to go meet Martin for one reason or another. I stood on the station platform as people brushed by me. But I wasn't quite ready to move.

I took a deep breath. It seemed to me this "thing" we had built, this march, was either going to work spectacularly or fail on the same level. Maybe we were about to build an unforgettable pyramid in the sands of American history; maybe the whole effort would be a big bust, a failure that would result in a substantial setback for our Movement and a blow to Martin's national nonviolent civil disobedience leadership. There was no middle ground and no turning back. We had gone all in and now we would see if our bets paid off.

As I moved through the train station, I thought of that Sunday in February 1960 in the Baldwin Hills Baptist Church outside of Los Angeles. I thought of Martin's sermon, the one that changed my life. Because when Martin Luther King, Jr. preached about you personally, that is a life-changing event. He didn't mention me by name, of course, but he used bits of my past he had picked up in our conversation at my home two nights earlier—my parents' struggle as poor domestics, my legal abilities put to work chasing after recording royalties instead of justice, my lack of compassion for my downtrodden brothers—and read me the riot act. With his arsenal of powerful words, Dr. King poignantly painted a picture of my mother scrubbing floors and hoping for better things for her son while he recited Langston

Hughes' "Mother to Son." I sat in the pew with tears streaming down my face. As he quoted from memory, "Life for me
ain't been no crystal stair," I felt like I had been pierced in
the heart with an arrow. Was I the son my mother deserved?

And from that point on, I was a Martin Luther King, Jr.
disciple. I joined him in Alabama. I gleefully helped Judge
Delaney and his superb team of defense lawyers destroy the
obviously trumped-up tax evasion charge.

I had gone from the willfully blind comfort of my living room in Southern California to the sticky air of the District of Columbia's Union Station and the March on
Washington in only three short years. I couldn't help pictur-
ing my mother again, smiling at me this time and saying,
"Clarence, you've come a long way, baby!"

I stepped out of the train station and into the muggy
summer night. There was no one in the cab line. I took a
Checker about a mile and a half to the Willard Hotel at the
corner of 14th Street and Pennsylvania Avenue. This was
where generations of D.C. power brokers plied their trade,
two blocks from the White House. Where we would work
on Martin's speech.

Several days earlier, Martin had told me he wanted Andrew Young, Walter Fauntroy, Ralph Abernathy, and Wyatt
Tee Walker to meet in the lobby of the hotel the eve of The
March. I'd asked him what the purpose was, and he said that
this was such "an important milestone in our civil rights
struggle," we should make every effort to get the best ideas of

those who worked so hard to make our March on Washington the success we assumed it would be.

Martin's response made me reflect on The March in
ways I had been too busy to think about before. What, indeed, was the true political and/or practical purpose of asking our supporters to gather by the thousands in Washington,
D.C.? Of course, I knew that in the mind of A. Philip Randolph—remember, not just the chairman of The March but
a virtual godfather of the entire Civil Rights Movement—
this was a march for jobs and freedom in roughly the same
vein as those earlier mass demonstrations he had led during
the Franklin D. Roosevelt Administration.

And then I thought about the very telling experience
Randolph had shared on various occasions with Bayard, Martin, Harry Belafonte, and others about one of his visits to the
White House when Roosevelt was president.[16]

After dinner, President Roosevelt asked Randolph to
share with him his views about the concerns and aspirations
of Negroes. Randolph was enormously grateful for the opportunity to discuss those issues directly with the president,
whose attention would empower his people. Accordingly, he
eloquently outlined an agenda for presidential action point by
careful point, underscoring the justice of his outlook, the economic value, and the moral fiber.

When Randolph completed his impassioned presentation, Roosevelt took a moment to process it all. Then he essentially told Randolph that he agreed with everything that he had said. It was stunning. And furthermore, the president said, he also agreed that as the leader of the nation, he had the political power to address many, if not all, of the issues they had just discussed.

Then, as the story goes, President Roosevelt turned to Randolph with a wry smile and said, "Now, go out and *make me* do it."

Roosevelt was suggesting that the issue wasn't one of right and wrong at all, of caring or not caring. It was about *leverage,* about power. It was the political version of the First Law of Thermodynamics. If Randolph organized and mobilized enough people to make the president feel the pressure to move on those issues of paramount concern to Negroes, then he would have no choice but to do so. But the same could be said of attempting to change any government policy, from the righteous to the trivial: If people do not organize to "make" our government do something, no change in policy will occur. The righteous policy and the trivial policy were interchangeable because they were both merely policy. Policy only responds to pressure. Take a look at the recent U.S. debacle in Iraq's Abu Ghraib prison. Torture was routine, and no one who knew about it had any intention of changing a thing until the pictures surfaced and got into the hands of an outraged public. That outrage moved policy mountains in the blink of an eye.

This story as Randolph told it was illuminating in its direct description of the process of power. That's what makes it seem novel, but it is really nothing new at all. The history of the African American struggle for freedom and equality in America has taught us again and again the wisdom of the abolitionist leader Frederick Douglass in his 1857 admonition:

> *Power concedes nothing without a demand.*
> *It never did and it never will.*[17]

In fact, isn't the Randolph mantra—"Nothing counts but pressure, pressure, more pressure"—just a modern twist on Douglass' teaching? Yes, I knew just where Randolph stood on the demonstration's meaning. But what did the milestone of The March symbolize for Martin and his leadership of the nonviolent direct action civil disobedience segment of the Civil Rights Movement? I thought about our failure to achieve our desegregation goals in Albany a year earlier, followed by Martin's successful struggle against the industrial citadel of segregation in Birmingham only nine months after that. Within this context I began to think of the March on Washington as a symbolic validation—even a *celebration*— of Martin's leadership of The Movement. If there were a significant number of people in attendance, especially people whose racial identity differed from Martin's, it would be a further and definitive statement that civil rights was not a Negro issue but an *American* issue.

CHAPTER TWO

TUESDAY

An Appeal to You from

MATHEW AHMANN

EUGENE CARSON BLAKE

JAMES FARMER

MARTIN LUTHER KING, JR.

JOHN LEWIS

ISAIAH MINKOFF

A. PHILIP RANDOLPH

WALTER REUTHER

ROY WILKINS

WHITNEY YOUNG

to MARCH on
WASHINGTON

WEDNESDAY AUGUST 28, 1963

America faces a crisis . . .

Millions of Negroes are denied freedom . . .

Millions of citizens, black and white, are unemployed . . .

We demand:
— Meaningful Civil Rights Laws
— Full and Fair Employment
— Massive Federal Works Program
— Decent Housing
— The Right to Vote
— Adequate Integrated Education

In your community, groups are mobilizing for the March. You can get information on how to go to Washington by calling civil rights organizations, religious organizations, trade unions, fraternal organizations and youth groups.

National Office —

MARCH ON WASHINGTON
FOR JOBS AND FREEDOM

170 West 130 Street   •   New York 27   •   FI 8-1900

Cleveland Robinson
Chairman, Administrative Committee

Bayard Rustin
Deputy Director

This flyer was one of the many grassroots methods the organizers used to spread the word about The March.

Photo courtesy Seth Kaller Inc.

When will our consciences grow so tender that we will act to prevent human misery rather than avenge it?

—Former First Lady Eleanor Roosevelt

EARLY SIGNS, EARLY WARNINGS

In the telephonic stone age that was 1963, as-it-is-happening information was quite hard to come by. The idea of knowing where anything or anyone was at any specific instance, this concept of "real time," had little meaning. But we did our best to work around that problem. If Ted Brown or another march organizer talked to a pastor from a particular church who said they had a bus leaving at 5:00 A.M., the information would be reported to Bayard or Martin. Then, perhaps ten hours later, the pastor would call again from a pay phone on the highway. "We're two hundred miles outside of Washington." It wasn't the same as tracking people with GPS, but it was the best we could do.

The same lack of information applied to the weather, which we were dreadfully worried about. These days if you're planning an outdoor party, the Weather Channel can give you a decent forecast ten days out. But in 1963, all we could do was call the National Weather Service incessantly. We would attempt to dredge up accurate information about Wednesday's weather at least twice a day. The forecast was always the same: Sunny with low humidity. But the mid-Atlantic summer could be fickle. I prayed the weathermen were right.

By midday on Tuesday, August 27, the calls really started coming in, a stream of them. "The plane just took off," or "The bus is full." And the forecast became more specific as we moved closer to the day of reckoning for The March. People were arriving and the weather remained favorable. That was the good news.

But something else unfolding was not nearly so uplifting. Tuesday afternoon we were made aware of a dispute between John Lewis and some other leaders of organizations participating in The March, including Archbishop Patrick O'Boyle of the Washington-area Catholic Diocese, a handful of labor leaders like Walter Reuther of the United Automobile Workers, and, just for good measure, the president's brother, the attorney general. Lewis, a future congressman but then the chairman of the Student Non-Violent Coordinating Committee, was, at 23, the youngest speaker on the program. He was angry and did not mind showing it. The dispute arose from a single paragraph near the close of his proposed speech that O'Boyle and the others regarded as provocative and potentially incendiary.

In my view, the entire text was provocative and incendiary, and, personally, I liked it that way. Lewis intended to create a hard-hitting spectacle, pointing out police brutality, the starvation wages for blacks, voter intimidation, and the glaring weaknesses in Kennedy's proposed Civil Rights Bill.

All that apparently was tolerable to the archbishop and his ilk. Sure, Robert Kennedy raised strenuous objections to Lewis calling the White House's Civil Rights Bill "too little, too late,"[1] but that was just the hurt feelings of a politician.

The *real* hard-core material seemed to pass without being re-marked upon. For example, there was no objection to the mention of the police officers who assaulted Marion King, the pregnant wife of Slater King, the attorney for our Albany, Georgia, Movement. And this attack caused Marion to mis-carry, which should be horrifying to any feeling person. But in the world of political rhetoric, symbolism is much more dangerous than detail. So, with his closing words, John Lewis wanted to draw an analogy that wasn't going to fly with some of the more politically oriented march organizers:

> *The time will come when we will not confine our marching to Washington. We will march through the South, the heart of Dixie, the way Sherman did. We shall pursue our own "scorched earth" policy and burn Jim Crow to the ground— non-violently. We will fragment the South into a thousand pieces and put them back together in the image of democracy.*[2]

This image of burning seemed to strike a chord of panic, the vision of Sherman's swath of fire too unsettling. The part where Lewis mentions that this was a *nonviolent* version of burning carried absolutely no weight.

Now, the Catholic churches in Washington, D.C. had been some of the earliest and strongest participants in support of The March. They had actively and openly encouraged their parishioners to attend. Furthermore, Archbishop O'Boyle was scheduled to deliver The March's invocation.

There was no alternative religious leader lined up, and the idea of starting The March without a blessing seemed foolhardy. The archbishop threatened to boycott the demonstration and to withdraw as a participating sponsor unless Lewis' speech was changed to eliminate the offending sentences. Reuther backed O'Boyle up with a similar ultimatum. Consequently, there was no question that Lewis' remarks would have to be sanitized so as to not upset Archbishop O'Boyle.

But Lewis led and served a constituency that demanded this kind of ferocious rhetoric. To get the young man to agree to change his speech would require genuine statesmanship. Cleve, Bayard, and I met and discussed the problem. Soon we realized that as dug in as Lewis was, even Martin didn't have the leverage to get him to soften his point of view. It seemed that, once again, the only one among us who could stand a chance of persuading Lewis to change the text of his prepared remarks was the pioneer of the enterprise, A. Philip Randolph. It was all up to him.

A GROUP OF LOBBYISTS

While the debate raged on over Lewis' controversial approach to getting his ideas across to the world, I headed back downstairs to the Willard's lobby. A crucial meeting was about to begin there.

The Willard Hotel was where many among the SCLC's march contingent were staying. It was also my hotel, and it was Martin's. Even before the meeting, I had spent a significant amount of my day in that lobby. We had no cell phones or BlackBerrys. Consequently, in order to conduct business, I had to make most of my telephone calls either from my hotel room or the pay phone in the main lobby area. I soon discovered that being sequestered in the hotel room was counterproductive. It was far easier to communicate with the other organizers, who were constantly coming and going though the hotel's revolving door, by positioning myself downstairs.

Those Martin asked to attend this final meeting to decide on the speech itself were Cleveland Robinson; Reverends Walter Fauntroy, Bernard Lee, and Ralph Abernathy; Professor Lawrence Reddick; Bayard Rustin; and me. I arrived downstairs a little early, but Martin and Ralph were already seated in a corner of the lobby, talking with some friends. As I approached, Martin politely told them we had several things to discuss related to the next day's march and his friends left. I spoke to one of the hotel bellmen and explained that we wanted to meet in the corner area Martin had already claimed, and we wanted to do so without any interruption. Martin was so well known there might be no work done that night if the usual parade of well-wishers were allowed access. The bellman was more than happy to help even before the ten-dollar bill hit his palm. After that I was able to convince the hotel management to give us a house phone patched through to an outside line that they could bill to my room.

When all of us had finally arrived, the bellman unofficially cordoned off the corner of the lobby—tables, chairs, and plants did the work of velvet ropes—to discourage people from coming over. I sat down, tired but enthused. I'd been dealing with endless logistics for days. It felt good just to sit and deal with a man and the one issue he was confronting. It felt, well . . . *civil.* I looked at the faces around the table. These were people who, like me, had spent the day working through the concrete organizational issues of The March. Now it was time to get to the heart of the matter. We were going to be asked our opinions about ideology, about the content of Martin's speech.

Wisely and without being asked, the bellman sent a waiter over from the restaurant. We ordered sandwiches and hors d'oeuvres to pass around. I thought about a martini but decided to pass on that for the time being. It was a good decision, because as the waiter departed, the serious business began.

A month or so earlier, Martin had decided to use this time on the eve of The March to map out his speech; he realized that with all the fine-tuning required for the various preparations, his confidants wouldn't be able to give his remarks their full attention until the last minute. Now it was the evening of Tuesday, August 27, 1963. With only a handful of working hours ticking away before the start of The March, there truly was nothing left to be done. It was time to focus on Martin's words.

Of course, in a broader sense, he certainly had not waited until the evening before The March to begin thinking about the nature of his address. First, he had a reservoir of concepts and scriptural material from speeches he'd given elsewhere. In addition, earlier that summer, before the deadline pressures were so intense, he had asked Wyatt, Bayard, and Andy for some thoughts on the tone and content of his speech. Then he and I had discussed the topics in more detail during the three weeks the King family spent at my home in Riverdale. After that, even more specifically, Martin had asked Stanley and me to prepare a draft of the point of departure, the direction, and the substance of some of the things we thought Martin should say.

I had brought along to Washington the draft text of Martin's speech that Stanley and I had crafted. It was in no way a final polished speech, but we had outlined some solid ideas. We believed that the occasion was a national extended mass meeting of our supporters. As such, we felt Martin had an obligation to provide leadership, offering a vision that we were involved in *action,* not *activity*; a clear-eyed assessment of the challenges we faced and a road map of how we could best meet those challenges. Ours was a speech built around new initiatives, and Martin had expressed enthusiasm when we'd presented it to him earlier in the month.

But the umbrella organization of the March Steering Committee was a reflection of broad-based support: Labor groups such as the UAW and the Teamsters and religious organizations of Catholics, Episcopalians, Methodists, Lutherans, Jews, and Greek Orthodox; community and civil rights organizations like the NUL, CORE, NAACP, SNCC, and the SCLC; and leaders from major secular and religious colleges and universities. So it was that Martin, showing how politically astute he was, now solicited specific views and ideas from a cross-section of his advisors beyond simply Stanley and me.

Martin initiated our discussion by mentioning that several of us had spoken to him or had given him notes on points he should make in his speech. He said he appreciated all of our thoughts and that he just wanted to review the ideas again and get the best approaches regarding the theme of his speech from those of us in attendance. What he *did not* say, though I believe strongly that he was thinking it (as was I), was this: Putting together these various concepts from the people gathered together would be difficult. The ideas would never hang together as a cohesive, thematic whole. Martin would have to take one approach—his own—with the rest of the ideas working in support of the larger theme's framework. He was far too diplomatic and kind to say it, but some of the people gathered would find their ideas littering the cutting-room floor before the evening was out.

Sitting in the lobby of the Willard Hotel, it was clear that Martin was genuinely interested in hearing the ideas and points of view of those assembled. Suggestions tumbled out.

"I think you should—" "Why don't we—" "Martin, as I mentioned before—"

For the first few minutes, Martin tried his best to sort out the blast of voices. But he lost patience quickly enough. He had intended this to be a session of thoughtful questions and the ideas those questions bring forth. But it seemed everyone had a stake in this speech, a predetermined angle. Martin looked over at me and said, "Clarence, would you mind taking some notes?" He suggested that when we were finished, I could organize them into something cohesive.

I wished silently for Dora McDonald, Dr. King's personal secretary, who had proven invaluable as an organizing force. She was the one who helped make sense of the handwritten scraps of newspaper and pieces of toilet tissue I had smuggled out of Martin's cell that became the "Letter from a Birmingham Jail."[3] If anyone could organize Martin's thinking, it was Dora. But Dora was on vacation, and I was on my own.

So, for the next few hours, I tried my best to keep track of all the information being offered up, discussed, and debated. I don't recall the exact order of who spoke first. Martin at some point acknowledged that he had already received written notes and suggestions from Wyatt Tee Walker and from Andy Young. Both were in and out of the meeting because of their other responsibilities in connection with The March, and both used our improvised "hot line" often.

Ralph Abernathy started getting at his main point, which seemed to be, "Martin, you have to preach. Most of the folks coming tomorrow are coming to hear you *preach*."

That was debatable. There were plenty of people in America who were more impressed with cogent social philosophy than with Baptist fire and brimstone. But after some discussion, it seemed to us all that what Ralph was trying to touch on was the concept of *inspiration*. Everyone thought Martin had to be, above all else, inspiring. Hey, pop the champagne, we had agreed on something!

But not everyone there defined "inspiring" in the same way.

That was a problem, because Ralph's idea of inspirational preaching did not match Wyatt's nearly mathematical approach regarding the "wrongness" of segregation, Bayard's call to action, or even my own "speak truth to power" ideologies. As it turns out, what a person finds inspiring depends largely on the person.

Cleve, Lawrence, and I, for example, saw the occasion of Martin's address as a major opportunity to stake an ideological and political "marker" in the national landscape of debate and discussion about civil rights. We favored a strategy to frame the national debate on racial segregation in a way that played to The Movement's advantage. This approach aligned well with my earlier private discussions with Martin and the concepts Stanley and I had already prepared on his behalf. Others in the meeting were more inclined for Martin to give a speech similar to a church sermon—that is, one steeped in parables and sprinkled with quotations from the Bible.

Amazingly, for a Christian-based movement, even the Bible wasn't safe territory. Bayard and Lawrence saw the use of biblical verse as sometimes obfuscating the "real" concern, which in their opinion was the legal system. Criminalizing institutional racism would do far more to create a desegregated America than any quote someone could dig up from the New Testament, they argued.

Still others in the group wanted Martin's remarks to be especially oriented to black and white student participants in our Movement. After all, they maintained, this was what John Lewis of the SNCC was trying to represent. The March was about looking to the future.

I kept on taking notes, all the while wondering how we were going to turn this into a cohesive speech.

Discussing the idea of Martin preaching in the classic sense brought with it an attendant idea: The stereotype of a preacher's sermon running too long. Someone, Cleve or Walter, I can't remember who, used that as a springboard to ask Martin a few pointed questions. What decision had been made by the March Steering Committee about when Martin was scheduled on the dais? How much time had finally been allotted for him to speak?

They asked Martin about these issues, but the whole time they were looking at me for the answers. I reminded them that I had no new information beyond what Bayard had told me: Mr. Randolph had agreed to introduce Martin as the last speaker. He promised that Dr. King would have at least fifteen minutes to speak, and he would let him speak longer if the time was reasonably needed.

Bayard nodded to the group. It was definitely news to some. Now we were all on the same page. We all knew Martin was the grand finale. It made our work in this meeting all the more important. Now, of course, came the question: What exactly was the man going to say?

One of the concerns periodically mentioned by Martin and others at the Willard Hotel lobby meeting was the number of people who would show up at The March. We maintained this macabre private joke that we had extended an invitation to attend a national party in Washington and very few people would attend. This anxiety was reflected in the conversations Martin and others had been having over the previous few days and nights. It hung around our lobby meeting, an unwelcome specter, as we tried to come to a consensus.

All of us experienced mood swings over the hours— back and forth from exhilaration to pessimism. Naturally, we were excited by the possibility of creating something for which perhaps one of the largest crowds of people for civil rights in the history of the country might assemble. But that was balanced with a healthy dose of skepticism that far fewer people would actually attend. Attendance was not simply a matter of pride or a show of force. A public reflecting little support for our Movement would not only be embarrassing, it would be financially disastrous. The March Committee and the respective participating organizations had spent well beyond what we had raised, and the major shortfall could be balanced out only with the anticipated revenues from the sale of programs and other souvenirs.

After several hours of back-and-forth discussion, we at last received a phone call from a member of the Washington SCLC office with word about A. Philip Randolph's intervention with John Lewis and his speech. It had been hanging over all the organizers' heads, a situation that could realistically derail our demonstration. The verdict? Lewis had decided to maintain respectful solidarity with Randolph and had modified some elements of his speech. After a grueling hour or more where Lewis insisted on a word-for-word rendition of his speech and Randolph tried to get Lewis to alter those words in an effort to smooth the ruffled feathers of certain March participants, they were still deadlocked. Randolph, though elderly, was crafty and highly experienced in the psychological nuances of negotiation, and so tried a different approach. He pressed Lewis' emotional buttons by reminding Lewis and his SNCC team that he had worked toward this March most of his life. Randolph pleaded for them not to ruin it for him. For *him*. Brilliantly, he had not made his argument in the broad strokes about ideals and politics; he made it about *one* man, the man sitting across from them who had dedicated himself in total to the Negro struggle. This was poignant enough to have real leverage. Lewis knew Randolph's original march had died when he was *one year old,* and that Randolph had been fighting for Lewis' future and that of the next generation of blacks more so than his own. And to be the upstart who pushed it into collapse on the eve of its resurrection more than twenty years later was too much for even the fiery young Lewis to have on his conscience.

No, when Lewis looked at it from Randolph's emotional position, he was finally able to open up to the idea of some level of compromise in his presentation. In another few hours, word got around that a satisfactory speech had been ironed out. Excised were the offending words that criticized the president's bill as being "too little, too late." Lost was the call to march through "the heart of Dixie, the way Sherman did." Gone was the too-reasonable question asking "Which side is the federal government on?" The word "cheap," used to describe some political leaders, was also deleted from the speech.

Archbishop O'Boyle would open the ceremonies after all.

In the end, when John Lewis stood at the lectern in front of all those people, his words would be slightly blunted. But the provocative voice with which he delivered them left no doubt regarding the young man's intended message, his fiery stance on the treatment of his people. His constituents remained well served by his words. The revised crescendo of John Lewis' speech as it was delivered will live on in history:

We will not stop. If we do not get meaningful legislation out of this Congress, the time will come when we will not confine our marching to Washington. We will march through the South, through the streets of Jackson, through the streets of Danville, through the streets of Cambridge, through the streets of Birmingham. But we will march with the spirit of love and with the spirit of dignity that we have shown here today.

By the force of our demands, our determination and our numbers, we shall splinter the desegregated South into a thousand pieces and put them back together in the image of God and democracy.

We must say, "Wake up, America. Wake up!" For we cannot stop, and we will not be patient.[4]

The incident with John Lewis was just one example of some of the undercurrents of differences between those assembled with Martin in the corner of the Willard lobby. And like the situation with Lewis and the archbishop, it was time for a compromise among these passionate men.

Martin said to me, "Clarence, why don't you excuse yourself and go upstairs. You can summarize the points made here and return with an outline of those key points and issues discussed. And, yes, try to do this without too many martinis."

It was probably somewhere between 9:30 and 10:00 P.M. when I left the group and went upstairs to my room to do as Martin requested. The plan was to write up an approach for his March on Washington speech, something that he could review, reflect upon, and make his own. I felt comfortable with that level of responsibility. If I had known how it was going to turn out, though, I'm not sure I would have exited the lobby so calmly.

MEMORY AND METAPHOR

A typewriter shouldn't have been too much to ask for, but there wasn't a Smith-Corona in sight. Fortunately, my style then (as it is often today) was to write my thoughts in parochial school longhand on a yellow legal pad. I sat at the desk in my hotel room, scrawling my way through the sheets of lined paper, trying to find my "in," my way to clarify the heart of our struggle. Mindful of what Martin had asked me to do, I tried to summarize the various points made by all of his supporters in the lobby. It was not easy; voices from every compass point were ringing in my head. Abernathy's conservative stance, Bayard and Cleve's take-no-prisoners call to arms, all of them with their tiny slice of a way to look at a large problem. There was justice, there was religion, there was compassion, and there was self-determination. I wrestled internally to find some way to pin down the right balance of celebration of achievements and goals yet to achieve.

I took out the material I had prepared earlier in the month with Stanley and reexamined it. I focused on the fact that we'd discussed coming to Washington not just to voice obvious complaints but with specific, actionable *demands*.

This had been a linchpin idea behind The March; Bayard's *Organizing Manual* even had a heading entitled "What We Demand." I toyed with the concept of making a demand of someone else, of the legal aspects, the personal aspects, and the vast gulf between the two.

As an example of a possible opening, I crafted an analogy of the Negroes marching to Washington to redeem a promissory note or a check for justice and freedom that had been handed back to us, marked "insufficient funds."

I also compared those points to the direction of the text Stanley and I had suggested and tried to blend the two sets of ideas and information together. Something worked its way up from the depths of my subconscious.

It wasn't a purely academic exercise in analogy. Four months earlier, during the Birmingham campaign, I had had a very successful meeting with New York governor Nelson Rockefeller. It concerned the effort to raise bail money for the youngest jailed protestors, whose parents were putting a lot of pressure on the SCLC to free them.[5] The Rockefeller family's history of concern over minority rights was well known. In fact, Spelman College was funded by his family and christened with Nelson's mother's maiden name as a thank you. Aside from the name, though, the Rockefellers were fairly quiet about their participation in The Movement. Whether that was a kind of humble, just-doing-what-is-right attitude or something a little bit more underhanded (there's a good chance the people the family did business with might not want to deal with a bunch of bleeding hearts), I cannot say. But I respected their sense of propriety and justice. Nelson Rockefeller's attitude back then was the very soul of the well-worn and oft-misused phrase "compassionate conservatism."

Even the most cavalier student of American history knows that Martin King ended up imprisoned in the Birmingham city jail in the spring of 1963, and the "hows" and "whys" are not the subject of this book. But something that has been missed in the ongoing historical excavation is a fascinating issue of economics. Just how was the SCLC able to make good on its promise to bail out the schoolchildren whose parents would never allow them to stay in jail when we did not have enough money to cover even a fraction of the unanticipated number of protesters locked up by Birmingham's notoriously brutal public safety commissioner "Bull" Connor? A good friend once told me, "It seems like you were the bagman of the Civil Rights Movement." He meant it as a compliment, I'm sure, but either way he was exactly right. Along with Stanley Levison, my role in The Movement—just as in my Wall Street work—was to make it rain.

Martin famously spent several gut-wrenching days in solitary confinement, but by the time I had gotten in to see him, he had been allowed back into the large, crowded holding cell. Solitary had been an intense experience. Martin King may have been a man whose very personality was forged by the discipline of Christian faith, but he was not unafraid in that cell. Fear is something so primal it cannot be willed away by anything as man-made as sheer discipline. That experience didn't make him a frightened man, but the anxiety and dread touched Martin easily because he loved life, and he knew how tentative its continuation might be for a person in his position. But solitary confinement also forced him to focus on these things in a way that his everyday life didn't allow. Though it was unnerving to Martin, it fed the flame of his spirituality and nourished—emboldened—his soul.

While in jail, Martin had been given a copy of *The Birmingham Herald,* the local newspaper that ran the now-infamous so-called open letter signed by eight white Alabama clergymen. In reality it was a full-page paid advertisement, one harshly critical of Martin's techniques for trying to effect change in the South. It was an attempt at appeasement by the city's white religious establishment upon personally witnessing the power of The Movement. The ad read, in part:

> *In Birmingham, recent public events have given indication that we all have opportunity for a new constructive and realistic approach to racial problems.*
>
> *However, we are now confronted by a series of demonstrations by some of our Negro citizens, directed and led in part by outsiders. We recognize the natural impatience of people who feel that their hopes are slow in being realized. But we are convinced that these demonstrations are unwise and untimely.*[6]

That outsider was my friend and, more importantly, a legal client. For that reason, while he was in jail, I alone among those involved with the SCLC was allowed to see him.

When I finally reached him, he pushed the newspaper at me, agitated. "Have you seen this?" he demanded.

I told him I had not. "I've been tied up raising funds, Martin," I explained. But I looked over the ad there in the jail cell. When I finished, I pointed out that it was cowardly bullshit. But I had to agree that, if the statements went unanswered, they had the potential to adversely influence white people of goodwill throughout the country. Yes, a timely response to the white clergymen's ad was a good idea. But I have always known that you have to put out the fire closest to you, so I had to share with Martin my concern (as well as Stanley's) regarding the potential impact on his leadership if we could not provide sufficient bail for the young demonstrators who had followed and joined him in incarceration. Mothers were screaming for us to get their kids out of jail and back to school, and we did not have the money to honor our promise.

Martin understood and acknowledged the seriousness of the bail issue but seemed far more concerned about—almost distracted by—the newspaper ad. It eclipsed his attention. "I have to answer this," he said.

Now I noticed for the first time what Martin had done to his copy of the newspaper. The margins were black with his scribbling. His manifesto. I knew what it was like, that feverish rush of ideology coming out of the point of a pen—

or, in this case, the broken nub of a pencil. The eight white clergymen had truly upset Martin, and this was a man who had been nothing but forgiving when he had faced down fire hoses and police dogs or been stabbed in the chest while autographing books.

"Take this out of here," Martin whispered, opening my suit coat and stuffing the pages in my waistband. "Have Dora type it up, okay?" I thought it was crazy, but I *was* his lawyer and a close friend. I began hiding the crucial sheets of newsprint where I could.

This mish-mash of words and arrows connecting them would one day become the "Letter from a Birmingham Jail," a document in American social history up there with the Declaration of Independence and the Bill of Rights. But I didn't know that then. All I knew was that there was newsprint and toilet paper stuffed under my shirt and down my pants, and Martin was not going to solve the bail money problem from inside a cell. It was up to me.

"See if you can smuggle some paper in for me tomorrow," Martin said.

I handed in the first scraps of what would turn out to be several days of Martin's writings to Dora and Wyatt Tee, the SCLC's chief of staff at the time.

"What am I supposed to do with this?" Dora asked.

"Treat it like anything else he hand writes and asks you to type," I said.

"Yeah, but he gives me those on lined paper. In *order*."

I offered a shrug. She knew exactly what to do. "Decode it," I said. "We'll see what it looks like in the morning."

From my room in the Gaston Motel, I called Harry Belafonte. It was the same call any of us has made a hundred times in our life. We have a money problem; we need someone to complain to about it. I wasn't asking for a solution, just a shoulder to support me while I worried aloud. I needed a sounding board while I sorted through what our options were for raising funds.

But Harry surprised me. "I have an idea," he said. "I think I can stir the pot. Let me do a little legwork. I'll get back to you."

The next day I returned to Birmingham Jail and was able to slip to Martin a legal pad, a pen, and Dora's typed-up draft. It wasn't exactly a file baked in a cake, but I have to admit I did some sweating as the guards debated on whether it was proper procedure to frisk a prisoner's attorney, something the other guards hadn't considered the previous day.

With paper and a pen Martin was able to make much better progress on his answer to the clergymen. Now even I could see the power of what he had in mind. No wonder he couldn't be bothered to worry about mundane bail issues. What amazed me was there was absolutely no reference material for Martin to draw upon. There he was, pulling quote after quote from thin air. The Bible, yes, as might be expected from a Baptist minister, but also British prime minister William Gladstone, Mahatma Gandhi, William Shakespeare, and St. Augustine.

Two days later, on Friday afternoon, I spoke to Harry again. He said he had been talking to Hugh Morrow, Governor Rockefeller's speechwriter, and there was an opportunity. He asked me to return to New York as soon as I could and instructed me to call Morrow at his home on Sutton Place "no matter what time your plane lands, Clarence."

It was late by the time I got off the plane, sometime after midnight. From the gate at LaGuardia, I called the phone number Harry had given to me. Morrow answered and said he'd been waiting for my call. If he'd been asleep or wanted to be, I couldn't sense it. It might as well have been two in the afternoon. "Mr. Belafonte tells me you and Dr. King have some difficulties down there. The governor and his family would like to be of help."

Be of help was—if you're a Carnegie, a Vanderbilt, a Rockefeller—a kind of upper-crust coded phrase interchangeable with this never-to-be-uttered-aloud sentiment: "How much do you need?" I hadn't asked Harry for money, but he had gone and asked someone else on my behalf. I suppose I have my coded phrases, too.

"Mr. Rockefeller and I would like for you to meet us tomorrow morning at the headquarters of the Chase Manhattan Bank on Sixth Avenue and Forty-seventh Street," Morrow told me.

I started to remind him that tomorrow was Saturday. This was 1963, and bankers' hours meant something very specific. No bank in the country was open for business on a Saturday. Then I remembered just whom I was talking to. The Rockefeller family owned this particular bank. He could probably walk into it at midnight on Christmas Eve if the desire struck him. I didn't quite know what to say. "Thank you" was as far as I got. It was a start.

"Save that for Mr. Rockefeller," he said. Then, thinking the better of it: "Actually, don't bother him with it either. We all know help is needed and appreciated."

Saturday there was a skeleton crew in the main branch of Chase Manhattan: A security guard, a banker, Hugh Morrow, Nelson Rockefeller, and me. Everyone would play his part: Rockefeller as the somewhat detached philanthropist, Morrow as the careful mouthpiece, the banker as the one making sure all the i's were dotted and t's were crossed, the Brinks agent with the gun making sure nothing went haywire. And me in the role of the hat-in-hand Negro, trying hard to appear as if this were not the strangest situation I had ever encountered.

It was more money than I had ever seen in one place before. Come to think of it, it was more stainless steel too. The thickness of that vault door was in perfect proportion to what it was guarding: Money stacked floor to ceiling. Literally. I was smart enough to know it was just paper, just a representation of something, not really the wealth itself, but, still, I had an almost primordial reaction to seeing all that currency. Some genetic memory that tells you money is freedom flushed adrenaline into my system. I stood there jittery with it as a banker counted banded stacks of bills into a brand-new briefcase. I was just starting to feel like I was going to get out of this in one piece and that I would return to Alabama a hero of The Movement when the confusion arose. As the security guard locked the briefcase, the banker handed me a single sheet of paper.

"Please sign this, Mr. Jones."

It was filigreed, and stamped with official-looking seals. In bold letters along the top it read: DEMAND PROMISSORY NOTE.

The banker saw the concern in my eyes. "Banking regulations, sir. It's . . . required."

I didn't have to be a banker to know what the paper meant. If I signed it, I became responsible for paying the money back. One hundred thousand dollars, in 1963, was worth more than seven hundred thousand dollars today.

"I can't personally promise this will be paid back."

"There are legal conditions that apply here," the banker said. "We need a signature or we can't release the funds."

I looked over at Rockefeller. "I don't have this kind of money, and neither does the SCLC."

"Just sign for it, Mr. Jones," Rockefeller said to me. "You don't need to worry about it."

Worried or not, I was out of choices. I thought of Martin, of all those kids in the jail missing school, and I scrawled out my name.

Remarkably, though Rockefeller never explicitly said so aloud, he would never make the demand for repayment. Nor would he leave me worrying. After everything was sorted out with the bail money in Birmingham over the weekend, I returned to my downtown Manhattan law office. The following Tuesday our receptionist buzzed to let me know a messenger was at our reception desk with something requiring my signature. He handed me an envelope from Chase Manhattan Bank marked "Personal and Confidential." Inside I found the one-hundred-thousand-dollar Demand Promissory Note I had signed on Saturday morning. Across its face was one red, rubber-stamped word: PAID.

Reflecting on that experience, I drafted the following to illustrate what Martin might consider saying to explain to the throngs why they had come to the March on Washington:

> *In a sense we've come to our nation's capital to cash a check.*
> *When the architects of our republic wrote the magnificent words*
> *of the Constitution and the Declaration of Independence, they*
> *were signing a promissory note to which every American was to*
> *fall heir. This note was the promise that men, yes, black men as*
> *well as white men, would be guaranteed the unalienable rights*
> *of life, liberty and the pursuit of happiness.*

*It is obvious today that America has defaulted on this
promissory note in so far as her citizens of color are concerned.
Instead of honoring this sacred obligation, America has given
the Negro people a bad check; a check which has come back
marked "insufficient funds."*

I had seen the cash nearly bursting out of the vault of the
Chase Manhattan Bank in New York. I knew wealth was out
there, and—Mr. Rockefeller not withstanding—I saw that
most wealthy people turned a blind eye to the hungry. The
same could certainly be said of the U.S. government and its
relationship to racism, uniquely positioned as it is with law-
making and -enforcing abilities. The government was rich
with the power to help us and utterly miserly in doing so.
They turned out empty pockets to show us there was nothing they could do.

Well, we would see about that.

"TO COUNSEL WITH MY LORD"

Martin Luther King, Jr. loved to write, but as his fame and
the demands on his time increased over the years, he found
he had fewer and fewer hours to write to the high standards
to which he held himself. It's telling that he did some of his
best writing in a prison cell, where all the distractions of day-
to-day life are held at bay.

Though he was without the time to prepare the kinds of
speeches he wanted to deliver, Martin was in the fortunate

position of having other people eager to write for him. He came to rely on me and Stanley as his draft speechwriters primarily because he trusted us to keep the facts about an issue straight and because, with our legal training, we had a way of presenting an argument with a polemic slant that went straight for the jugular. Our writing style worked within a careful structure and was designed specifically to sway opinions. However, it was not without its shortcomings on occasion. Martin used to kid me after he read a draft I'd offered, saying, "Clarence, it's as tight an argument as I can imagine, but where's the humanity?" When it came to my speech drafts, he often acted like an interior designer: I would deliver four strong walls and he would use his God-given abilities to furnish the place so it felt like home. So even though an hour and a half after I went up to my hotel suite I finally felt like the work was in order, I harbored no illusions about my ability to get the emotion of the issue across. I knew that perhaps I'd organized the basic principles, which was a difficult task considering all the differing opinions downstairs, but Martin would have to breathe life into them.

I collected those papers that weren't crumpled up in the corner by the overflowing trashcan and returned to the lobby. The participants were now more animated in their discussions than when I'd left, but I think it was the giddiness that comes with exhaustion. Their voices were shrill and worn out. Martin looked tired to me—more so than usual, and I saw him tired often.

I returned to my place in the loose arrangement of lounge chairs opposite Martin and waited to present the material. He asked everyone to be quiet and give their attention to what I was about to report. I had the floor. As requested, I gave a summary of what, in good faith, I truly believed to have been the essential points from the earlier discussion with Martin and the group. They let me go on for maybe three minutes, no more, when the group began to interrupt me.

"What about—"

"No, no, no, no—"

"Why didn't you—"

"I thought we *agreed*—"

They were all over me. One man after another claimed that either I had left out an important concept that had been made during the earlier discussion or had inaccurately summarized what had been said about any of a dozen particular points. And given the fact that several of the men there were Baptist preachers, there was no small amount of grandstanding and finger-wagging.

This reaction took me off guard. I began to defend my work and respond to those who challenged the accuracy of my summary.

But I didn't get very far. Martin intervened. "Okay, brothers," he said, "thank you so much everybody for your suggestions and input." He singled me out as I handed him my handwritten sheets of paper. "Clarence, I want to thank you for your efforts."

I nodded my appreciation as Martin stood up. He had been in that chair for nearly six straight hours.

"I am now going upstairs to my room to counsel with my Lord," he announced. "I will see you all tomorrow." He turned to me one last time and told me that someone would be in touch with me in the morning to share his completed speech.

And then he walked quietly out of the room and made his way to the elevators, leaving the rest of us to look at each other for just a moment. "Tomorrow, then," someone said, and we dispersed.

I took a breath. Pictured the bed waiting for me upstairs. Then retreated to the lobby bar alone and ordered an ice-cold gin martini, a small signal to myself that my work was done. I held the glass, its inverted construction an insult to gravity and the order of things. Just like our Movement, from the outside the balance of power seems all wrong. But hold a martini glass in your hand and you know instinctively that it is just right.

I signed the check and then went upstairs to my room to try to get what little rest I could.

CHAPTER THREE

WEDNESDAY

Dr. King with Stanley Levison and an unidentified associate.

Photo courtesy the estate of Stanley Levison

I went out drinking with Thomas Paine
He said that all revolutions are not the same
—Billy Bragg,
"North Sea Bubble"

DAWN RECONNAISSANCE

Early, about 7:00 A.M., my hotel room phone rang. I had to drag myself out of a deep sleep to answer. It was Martin's secretary on the line, the woman filling in for Dora MacDonald. She told me Martin's speech had been completed. If I had been more awake I would have felt surprised, because it hadn't been that many hours since I had handed in the outline and, like me, Martin had to be exhausted. But apparently it was done. I told her that it was great news.

"It's being mimeographed now," the secretary said to me, explaining that The March organizer in charge of the press was going to insert a copy in each journalist press kit. This was a standard practice at lectures and speeches. It allowed newspaper writers to submit a significant portion of their coverage to their editor in advance of the event, which in turn helped ensure that the speaker received timely and accurate press coverage. Excellent, I thought, we're moving along. But as I hung up, something was nagging at me. I couldn't put my finger on what it was exactly, and I was exhausted and had a long list of tasks to handle. For the time being, I simply had to let it go. I showered and dressed and prepared myself to face the day.

When I stepped outside and discovered the sun and clear skies, I became energized. It looked as if the weather would cooperate with us after all. Then I turned my attention back down to Earth, across the ellipse, to the marchers I saw assembling on the Mall at the base of the Washington Monument. The crowd was increasing even as I watched it. People were joining, some holding placards that I couldn't read from my distance. I knew the soul of their messages, though. We were all here in support of the same ideals. It was heartening. We were giving that party, and people were actually showing up. Soon they would begin to march—not east to the Capitol steps as we had originally envisioned, but west to the Lincoln Memorial. There had been a change of plans.

Our march was being organized during the administration of President John F. Kennedy and his attorney general brother, Robert. They were not quite the astute politicians Roosevelt had been when discussing racial strife with A. Philip Randolph. Though we knew and accepted the idea that pressure, not presidential empathy, was the instrument of change, we still would have enjoyed an indication that JFK and his brother would welcome our march as an opportunity for us to "make them" act to forthrightly and immediately address those issues of civil rights and work opportunities of foremost concern to Negroes in 1963. There was no such indication. In fact, our original planned site for The March's finish line, the Capitol Building, which would have put us on the "making him" footing, was met with utter contempt from the White House. The president said his lawmakers would perceive this action as "putting a gun" to the collective head of the leadership of the Congress.

We had thought about this long and hard in the weeks leading up to The March. Holding a gun to the head of the government: Is that the image a nonviolent movement for civil rights and justice wanted to project? In the end, the offensiveness of this idea persuaded the organizers of the March on Washington to change the venue of the demonstration. In Bayard's update to his *Organizing Manual No. 1,* the finish line for the marchers was changed to the foot of the Lincoln Memorial. With its Mall and reflecting pool, its 180 acres of lawn, and its enormous reminder of the emancipation of the nation's slaves, it would prove to be a brilliant move.

But looking across at the Washington Monument, I felt a darker sensation running through me as well. In the same way that my first glance of the marchers filled me with a sense that this demonstration would be larger than my capability to imagine it, my first glimpse of Washington's crowd control approach made me feel as if real trouble were in store. Troops were moving along Constitution Avenue, wedged between the early marchers and me like a fence.

Washington, D.C. seemed virtually under martial law. President Kennedy had ordered federal troops to duty and put nearby military bases on combat readiness alert. As I stood there, Hoover's agents were busy calling the hotel rooms of our roster of celebrities, trying to scare them into abandoning The March. In the end we never knew if any celebrities who had agreed to participate but changed their minds did so because of this pressure. The District's police force was approaching The March like an army approaches a battle. A front-page *New York Times* piece on city planning for The March that ran Monday, August 26, stated that "the operation is military in its precision and detail."[1] The downtown Washington area around the Mall had been divided into five police commands. Two-thirds of the District's police force had been assigned to The March. An internal police department memo was quoted in the *Times* article, calling Wednesday "the most important day in the history of the metropolitan police."[2] And that is not just any old city police force; we are talking about an organization that routinely has to deal with inaugurations, visiting royalty, and demonstrations of all stripes.

In his book *The Civil Rights Movement: A Photographic History, 1954–68,* Steven Kasher points out, "the main rally would be at the Lincoln Memorial. For the organizers, that site had a powerful symbolism, particularly on the centennial of the Emancipation Proclamation. The police liked the site because, with water on three sides, the demonstrators could be easily contained."[3]

The absurdity of a Gandhi-influenced Christian leader of a nonviolent ethos needing to be forcibly contained seemed lost on D.C.'s finest. Why the high tension? Despite the fact that March organizers had called a press conference mainly to underscore the peaceful ideals embraced by The Movement, the government's concerns over the potential out-break of violence remained. They *hoped* for a peaceful day but they had to be *prepared* for a war. At that press conference, the Washington leadership of the SCLC and other Movement leaders pledged that the marchers would be:

> *Orderly, but not subservient*
> *Proud, but not arrogant*
> *Nonviolent, but not timid*
> *Outspoken, but not raucous*[4]

Regardless of our intent, the authorities were gearing up for the worst. The idea was that a show of force would both act as a deterrent to violence as well as the potential means to handle it. Some of the results of this bunker mentality were indicated in Kasher's book, where he offers a chilling run-down of the District's preparations, including: Special riot-control training given to adjacent suburban police forces; all leaves canceled for District police officers; liquor sales banned the day of The March for the first time since the repeal of Prohibition; the Justice Department and the army coordi-nated preparations for emergency troop deployments; fifteen thousand paratroopers put on alert; and a crew of lawyers convened to prepare proclamations authorizing military action *in advance.*[5]

On the other hand, the government also dreaded the potential for any bad press that would follow on the heels of these hypothetical riots. For example, because of the adverse worldwide reaction to newspaper photos and television news video of German shepherds attacking civil rights demonstrators in Birmingham four months earlier, Attorney General Kennedy decided to ban police dogs at The March (nevertheless, there were plenty of photos on various handmade placards to remind the world).

As a result, those in authority walked a fine line between looking as if they were against The March and acting as if they welcomed its peaceful execution. This led to subversive behavior. For example, the Justice Department and the police had worked hand in hand with the March Committee to design a public address system powerful enough to get the speakers' voices across the Mall; what March coordinators wouldn't learn until after the event had ended was that the government had built in a bypass to the system so that they could instantly take over control if they deemed it necessary.

Now, that is a fairly well-known story at this point, and there are those out there who believe it's an unproven rumor. I think the record on the issue should be cleared. Martin did not concern himself much with the on-the-ground logistics of the execution of The March. Consequently, I wasn't very involved in a hands-on way, either. This was the principal concern of Ted Brown, with Bayard supervising it all. Ted, along with Cleve, rounded up members of the various participating labor unions to erect the speakers' platform, the podium, and the sound system.

Ted had developed a close working relationship with several Negro officers in the D.C. Police Department and a couple of staffers from the Justice Department in support of his efforts on behalf of The March. Both Ted and Bayard told us that right after The March ended those officers approached them, eager to relieve their consciences and reveal the truth about the sound system. There was a kill switch and an administration official's thumb had been on it the entire time.[6]

SO TIRED OF ALL THE EXPLOITATION

I had celebrities to meet, but I decided to head for the press area. I'd just figured out what had been bothering me about the organization's plan to distribute copies of the speech to all the attending members of the press.

Many times in the past I had witnessed images of Martin or excerpts of his work being used to promote all manner of commercial or political agendas. Naturally, neither he nor the SCLC received any benefit from these promotions. This time, I planned to make sure that didn't happen.

Martin's image and voice were like logos companies could stamp on their products. Everyone wanted a piece of him. I always found it interesting that he had achieved his stature by acting selflessly, and it was this stature that was being used for selfish personal gain. Martin was a man of great patience, of course, and he put up with this time and time again.

I always made it as clear as I could, constantly telling him, "They're using you, you know."

And though he understood this, he did not particularly mind. But I saw it as a hustle, and it rubbed me the wrong way every time.

Martin and I were opposites in many ways. The discipline of patience was one of those ways. I had no patience at all for this misappropriation of his name, likeness, and work. And one of the things I have always been very good at is speaking out on behalf of my friends.

I have come to think of law school as a kind of cerebral analog to the physical process a recruit goes through in the basic training portion of the armed services. For better or for worse, I've gone through both experiences. And the parallel is simple. In the military, the people in charge do not want individuals; they want to make every soldier into the ideal. They physically melt you down and recast you at the absolute limits of your strength and endurance. The exact same process happens in legal training, but to your mind. You have to make it through a grueling educational process, but once you do, you are primed to view the world through new eyes. You are not emotional, you are not afraid. Still, you cannot help but see the potential pitfalls and downsides in every interaction. It is a cautionary mind-set they hand you on graduation day, and you cannot get rid of it even if you want to.

And now, even though I had not done so with previous speeches, my instincts were telling me to look at the dissemination of the Washington speech to the press in just this way: Wait a minute, what do we stand to lose here?

One of my limited areas of specialty as a lawyer at that time was copyright law. I knew well the clear distinction between common law and statutory copyright protection as well as legal issues involved. At that time, people had a proprietary right, in most states, to own and control their intellectual creations embodied in words they had written. Retention of common law copyright, which amounted to a simple indication on copies of the work, would qualify an author to apply for subsequent statutory copyright protection under the United States Copyright Act. However, if the owner of a common law copyright widely disseminates his writing without notice of common law copyright protection, this can be deemed to effect a "publication," extinguishing the author's common law copyright and in turn disqualifying him from registering his writing for statutory copyright protection.

Traditionally how it worked in the public speaking and press game was that people making a speech, if they even understood the ownership value of intellectual property at all, traded that value away on the assumption that the value of the press coverage for the appearance was of greater value than potential copyright profits. I didn't want that to happen to whatever Martin planned on saying at the close of the March on Washington, and the one thing I was sure would be happening at the press tent would be people handing out copies of his speech.

HOW DO YOU KNOW YOU'RE MAKING HISTORY?

As I pointed out in the opening pages of this book, I truly neither want nor take any real credit for the value of the intellectual property the copyright provided. Like many of both my best and worst decisions over the years, the decision to copyright Martin's speech was fueled mostly by a sense of frustration and vague anger with just a dash of paranoia thrown in. And as a man who has in the intervening years learned that he was under around-the-clock illegal government surveillance, I think paranoia is sometimes undervalued.

I wasn't thinking about the upside, I was thinking defensively. And when I did finally get around to considering the upside, it's almost embarrassing how off target I was. My goal was to protect, not to profit, and it was the culmination of a number of feelings that I could not subsume no matter how hard I tried. I was sick and tired of watching people take advantage of Martin's easygoing nature. His open heart. I had a strong feeling it could happen again here. He was going to give his ideas away, and I knew other people were going try to make money off those ideas.

It's not that the speech itself seemed so important on paper. I would be lying to myself if I claimed that kind of foresight. I hadn't read it, for one thing. It was more the sense that The March would have a reverberating impact, and Martin Luther King, Jr.'s speech would be a tangible by-product. It would be recorded and reproducible. In essence, it was something concrete to which he could lay claim.

And so I made my way to the March Committee's "News Headquarters," a gigantic tent near the Lincoln Memorial we'd put up to make sure reporters received all the information they needed about the day. I found some volunteers there working. Martin's speech was being mimeographed, stapled, and inserted in large envelopes comprising the press kits for the journalists at The March. I picked up one of the copies lying in a pile on a table. Sure enough, it did not contain any notice of copyright protection. This did not surprise me, of course. We'd never before affixed that little circled "c" on press copies of his previous speeches. What surprised me was that I was suddenly thinking about it.

Reporters and photographers were everywhere. According to Kasher, "Press coverage for The March was more extensive than for any previous political demonstration in U.S. history. The committee issued no fewer than 1,655 special press passes."[7]

It felt like even more from the trenches. Forget for a moment the newspapers that would be running at least parts of the speech; the mere distribution of the work to this many members of the press could potentially constitute a publication, the last thing you wanted when trying to maintain common law copyright protection.

However, preempting the newspapers' first publication rights did not mean that the papers could not run the speech. It only meant that the rights were still retained. All it would take was a little elbow grease. Why not be sure that the mimeographed copies of Martin's speech in the press kits contained a common law notice of copyright? I knew the smart move would be to retrieve the copies of the speech from the press kits and handwrite a symbol of a small circle with a "c" inside on each page of each copy. So I introduced myself to the people who seemed to be in charge of assembling and distributing the press kits and told them what I wanted to do.

They told me what I could do with my idea.

But I think the sheer determination on my face got through to them, and my raised voice alerted others with a little more authority who were on the far side of the tent. Someone came over and recognized me. He mentioned to the people I was arguing with that I was "Dr. King's New York lawyer." That changed everything. My request suddenly didn't seem so intrusive and my instructions were followed. Several young volunteers grabbed ballpoint pens and started scribbling the appropriate copyright notice on each page of each copy of the speech.

I did my share of the work as well. I flipped through many copies of the three-page speech, making the little circled "c" like everyone else. My attention was divided, though. I needed to reconnect with Harry Belafonte to learn the logistics of the celebrity delegation's arrival by plane from California around noon. Harry had asked me to assume responsibility for meeting all the celebrities and directing them to their reserved section in the stands near the podium. I was so distracted thinking about how I was going to be able to reach him that as I worked the strokes of the letter "c" and the circle on all those pages, I still did not think to read the final text of what Martin had written. It just wasn't my principal concern, and it's not as if someone were tapping me on the shoulder to tell me I should pay attention, that I was in the middle of an incredibly historic day.

I gave no further thought to Martin's speech that morning. Instead, I turned my attention to coordinating with Harry and helping with the celebrities. The next time I saw a copy of that speech, it would be on the lectern in front of Martin Luther King, Jr.

'BUKED AND SCORNED

By about ten o'clock, a large number of marchers had gathered at the stage we'd constructed at the base of the Washington Monument. The March leaders, who also constituted the vast majority of the speakers, were lobbying on the Hill, so there had to be something going on before the speech program began. That something was music.

Harry made sure Joan Baez, Bob Dylan, and many other towering musicians provided a vibrant soundtrack to The March. Joan took to the stage with a rousing version of "Oh Freedom" then topped it with the moving and apt "We Shall Overcome." The lyrics to Dylan's "Blowing in the Wind" had become like a clarion call for the Civil Rights Movement. Interestingly, though Dylan was in attendance (as was Peter, Paul and Mary, whose "Blowing in the Wind" cover was getting tremendous airplay at the time), neither act took on the song. Pete Seeger ended up performing "Blowing in the Wind." Dylan's original recording is transcendent, of course, but I will always have a soft spot for Seeger's sultry rendition. As a type—an activist barely disguised as an artist—Seeger always showed support for social justice in all forms. His dedication was legendary then and remains so to this day. Josh White was another memorable act that day. Bayard was old friends with him. In fact, multi-talented man that he was, Bayard had played guitar in Josh's band years before. I made a point of slowing down long enough to hear a song or two from his set.

While the musicians played, the crowd swelled. When it was all over, the estimates of the crowd size I saw ran the gamut: from a low of 200,000 (too low in most people's opinion, even many of our detractors') to a half million (impossibly high). Either way, it was going to be considered a remarkable success.

There were, naturally, a few notable travel stories that the press picked up on: A small group of CORE members took nearly two weeks to walk from New York to Washington, and a trio of teenagers from Alabama hitchhiked, arriving much earlier than they'd anticipated. For the most part, though, it was buses and trains streaming in all morning.

Robert Parris Moses, an officer in SNCC at the time, loved picketing. One of his early civil rights actions involved picking up a sign to protest small businesses' discrimination policies, and he said at that moment he suddenly "felt very free."[8] Moses apparently couldn't wait for The March to start. On Tuesday, August 27, the day before, he protested in front of the Justice Department Building (now named the Robert F. Kennedy Justice Department Building) with a hand-painted picket sign. It was a precursor to what I would see on the Mall the next morning. As I had predicted, many of the marchers made their own signs and some even wrote on their clothing. I knew there was no way some pamphlet was going to tell this crowd of excited protestors how to express themselves. Bayard's *Organizing Manual No. 1* was clear in its prohibition against people making their own placards. He had allowed for certain organized groups—labor, religious, fraternal, and sponsoring organizations—to make their own "signs of identification," but leaving the wholesale thematic ideas to individual marchers seemed careless:

> Slogans: All slogans carried in this March will be designed ex-
> clusively by the National Committee and will be distributed
> at the Washington Monument.[9]

Not quite. Slogans about murder, for example, were com-
monplace, and that was definitely not March Committee language. The people here felt free to express their anger and
frustration in individual, sometimes strident, ways. But the
official slogans didn't pull many punches, either. I studied the
various official placards being handed out, and noticed the
theme of *making demands* that I'd used as a starting point in
the previous night's draft of the speech was echoed in many
of them:

> *We Demand Decent Housing Now*
> *We Demand Equal Rights Now*
> *We Demand An End To Bias Now*
> *We Demand Voting Rights Now*
> *We Demand An End To Police Brutality Now*

Indeed, a sign didn't need the word to get the message across
that we were in a demanding frame of mind. Kasher describes
in his book a young black woman with a sign that read, "Not
'Negroes' But Afro-Americans! We Must Be Accorded Full
Rights as Americans Not in the Future but Now."[10] This sign

is one I didn't see, but I appreciate how utterly prescient her inspiration was. Twin demands, one of which, at any rate, seems to have been granted.

The music was gratefully absorbed by the crowd for some time, but as the hours passed, impatience began to take hold. Before the official 12:00 P.M. starting time for The March, I was making my way through the crowds to meet Charlton Heston. I was approached by some of the union men I knew from New York who were serving as marshals and essentially working crowd control. They told me that some of The March attendees who'd arrived early had taken matters into their own hands and had begun to march toward the Lincoln Memorial. Others followed, and before the marshals knew it, The March had started all on its own.

Martin and the other leaders, still on Capitol Hill, got word of the situation soon enough. They found themselves hustling through the crowd, trying to get to the front line so they could be seen ceremoniously leading The March. A few quick-thinking marshals pushed ahead, separating the shoulder-to-shoulder crowd like offensive linemen clearing the way for a quarterback's run so the leadership could make progress. Given the circumstances, they made it to the front of The March as quickly as anyone could have hoped. The cameras snapped and whirred. The leaders led. It was a literal "come from behind" victory.

As political strategists, we knew the importance of image as a tool. Just as being seen at the head of The March was critical to the image of the civil rights leaders, we knew elected officials felt that under certain circumstances, being seen by their public was important. Using the time-honored political tactic of pressure, we had cordoned off an area right by the main stage reserved for key government officials. Reserved by *name.* We made it clear that the world would know whose name was on any empty seats. I'm proud to say every one of those folding chairs was filled, though it's likely in some cases they were filled not by the officials they were intended for but by a staffer. To this day no one knows for sure. Politics can be an amazingly subtle game.

The audience was able to get the female perspective for the most part only from the women singers that afternoon. Opera singer Marian Anderson was supposed to lead the national anthem, but she was running behind schedule and missed the timeslot. Instead, Camilla Williams was able to step in on almost no notice and perform a beautiful rendition of a notoriously difficult song.[11] Joan Baez, as I mentioned earlier, stirred the crowed, as did other female singers. Songs communicate emotions, and their work was key. But in terms of the discourse on the racial environment at the time, the women were virtually exiled from the podium. Expatriate Josephine Baker was the sole female allowed on the speakers program. Not Daisy Bates, president of the Little Rock chapter of the NAACP, not even Rosa Parks, though both were in attendance. During the planning stages, we had argued over the role women would play in The March. Ted Brown periodically brought up the question of their participation. When I first heard about the issue, I had an immediate reaction that I kept to myself. I believed that most of the women in The Movement at that time had to contend with a kind of religious glass ceiling—a glass steeple, you could call it. Women of course, were, as they are today, a major part of the membership of most Black Churches. Yet except for the Pentecostal denominations, there were few women pastors of mainstream Methodist or Baptist churches. The Movement was male dominated, and those males were ego-driven. There were certainly no female clergy members in Martin's Southern Christian Leadership Conference. In the end Bayard folded a "Tribute to Women" into the official March program. I didn't argue with this decision at the time. Looking back, however, I must say that choice was very much a slight to the concept of "equality for everyone," which was the true theme of our demonstration.

When Bayard introduced some of the prominent female civil rights workers (or, in some cases introduced the widows of civil rights martyrs), the crowd roared its acclamation and approval: Dorothy Height, president of the National Council of Negro Women; Fannie Lou Hamer, the Mississippi activist beaten and permanently injured by police; Dorothy Cotton, of Martin's SCLC; Gloria Richardson, of the Cambridge Movement. These women and many others had become household names within the civil rights struggle. There would have been interest in what they had to say, and I wish we'd given them that opportunity.

As someone who *was* entitled to speak—in fact, as the penultimate speaker who set the stage for Martin—John Lewis got his licks in. Though to his way of thinking his speech had been diluted, you wouldn't know it by the audience reaction. In his pictorial history of The Movement, Kasher writes: "[Lewis'] toned-down speech was received with unmatched enthusiasm; it was interrupted by applause fourteen times. When he finished, he walked past the other leaders on the platform. Every black hand reached out for his, while every white speaker sat still, staring into space."[12]

After all the artists had performed and all the speakers from the major participating organizations finished delivering their remarks came the moment everyone had been waiting for. The sun was shining brightly. The lawn around the Lincoln Memorial glowed and the giant rectangular reflecting pool shot glints of light in every direction. From my vantage point near the dais I could see thousands and thousands of people standing and clapping as they watched and waited. Others were still walking onto the grounds where the stage was located, showing up for the big finish.

Instead of Martin directly following Lewis, Mahalia Jackson took the stage, a bit of showmanship arranged to further increase the crowd's anticipation of the grand finale: The closing speech by Martin. Mahalia had a lovely, moving singing voice, but what made her a consummate entertainer was that she understood audiences. She could sense their mood from the stage, and she could make the right artistic choices in the moment because of this. She understood the dynamics of performer-audience intimately, a skill that was about to come in extremely useful to America.

Mahalia chose a traditional gospel piece, "I've Been 'Buked and I've Been Scorned." It is a spiritual of woe and hope like many others. At first glance. But consider this lyric:

> *Children, I've been 'buked and I've been scorned*
> *Tryin' to make this journey all alone*

This was the key—under oppression everyone feels alone, or at least vastly outnumbered. It was musical and social counterpoint, an emotional reminder of just how important the crowd was—not simply the ideas and actions, but the people—and it was beautiful.

In the introduction to Doris E. Saunders' 1963 book *The Day They Marched,* Lerone Bennett, Jr. boiled down Mahalia's performance that day to its transcendent nature: "The button-down men in front and the old women in back came to their feet screaming and shouting. They had not known that this thing was in them, and that they wanted it touched. From different places and different ways, with different dreams they had come, and now, hearing this sung, they were one."[13]

Mahalia galvanized the crowd that was already unified in its purpose. No more making the journey all alone, not when there are a quarter of a million of your brothers and sisters ready to stand with you. She had struck a spark and ignited something. And she wasn't done yet.

PREPARATION: THE SPEECH, PART ONE

It had been a long day. Exhilarating but exhausting, filled with emotion as well as reason, protest as well as prayer. But it was all winding down. The time was now at hand.

A. Philip Randolph moved slowly to the podium. He seemed all business, yet his eyes glistened as they swept over the anticipating faces of the marchers. Looking back, I can see exactly why Randolph was so thrilled. In a sense, he had had his own dream as well. And at that moment, in front of the endless wave of hopeful people, his dream had come true. He introduced Reverend Martin Luther King, Jr., and I could feel the tension and an air of anticipation as I watched the crowd spring to life. Randolph referred to Martin as "the moral leader of our nation." I was in complete agreement. In fact, he was talking about the man I believe saved me from my destiny as just another hardheaded man in pursuit of status and the almighty dollar.

When Martin stood up to make his way to the podium, the crowd tensed in unison, as if each person had instantaneously been transformed into part of one giant organic mechanism and each no longer had any individual purpose outside of attenuating to this specific action, the moment when their cause was given voice on the international stage by the most important black man in America. The thunderous sound of applause followed as Martin stepped up to replace Randolph at the podium. I was standing perhaps fifteen yards behind him and off to one side, so I had a slight angle. I could see the vast crowd in front of him, but more importantly, as I wasn't looking directly at the back of his head, I could see enough of his profile to register that he was smiling. The hum of excitement died down and a hush fell over the crowd. It was time for the closing address. The people who made the sojourn to The March *knew* his words would give them direction.

I was sure they would as well. They always had. I did not know what he was going to say, however; I still hadn't had a chance to review how he had incorporated my suggestions.

Martin offered a traditional ad hoc greeting to the people assembled. "Brothers and Sisters, I am happy to join with you today in what will go down in history as the greatest demonstration for freedom in the history of our nation." Then, glancing down at the first of the few typed pages he had placed on the podium before him, Martin began to speak:

> *Five score years ago, a great American, in whose symbolic shadow we stand today, signed the Emancipation Proclamation.*

This momentous decree came as a great beacon light of hope to millions of Negro slaves who had been seared in the flames of withering injustice. It came as a joyous daybreak to end the long night of their captivity.

But one hundred years later, the Negro still is not free.

I listened carefully to Martin's words as he moved into the body of the speech. For the first time, I learned what was typed on the papers before him. A pleasant shock came over me as I realized that he seemed to be essentially reciting those suggested opening paragraphs I had scrawled down the night before in my hotel room. This was highly unusual, given the way we worked together. And even though nothing in our three-year history indicated this would ever happen, I began to wonder if, with all Martin had going on, he just did not have time to review the work and merely had his secretary type up what I'd submitted late the previous night. If so, I thought, thank God I put my all into it, and thank God that, aside from the idea of the promissory note, the entirety of the material was directly taken from what I had come to think of as our "ideological toolkit."

This concept is very familiar to anyone who's worked in an arena where a central message needs to be communicated over and over, before numerous audiences of varying interests. Martin's philosophies and worldview were the wellspring of all the original thinking that went into the SCLC's leadership in The Movement, each a kind of building block.

The nonviolent approach to protesting, the idea that it is in the majority's own best interest that Negroes achieve equality, and the economic leverage of boycott are all examples. There were dozens of ideas, but it was a manageable number; a philosophical menu that you could wrap your head around. The challenge was the need to review and reorganize the concepts anew for each particular audience or narrowly focused speaking opportunity. We had to thread the right ones together like pearls on a strand. This made the task of drafting speeches a subtle affair. Take the opening lines of The March speech, for example. They are a subtle variation of what Stanley and I had suggested to Martin for a speech at the "Freedom Rally" at Detroit's Cobo Hall two months earlier. The words became: "Almost one hundred and one years ago, on September the twenty-second, 1862, to be exact, a great and noble American, Abraham Lincoln, signed an executive order, which was to take effect on January the first, 1863. This executive order was called the Emancipation Proclamation and it served to free the Negro from the bondage of physical slavery. But one hundred years later, the Negro in the United States of America still isn't free."

The support for Martin that Stanley and I undertook had always been pulling together the right few issues for a particular audience, arranging them in a suggested framework. And while he appreciated when we would suggest fully developed material, he always made it his own. We had our ongoing process. Together we would discuss the goal for a particular audience of an upcoming speech. Those ideas would usually lead to Martin's request that Stanley or, to a lesser extent, I attempt a draft. Once complete, Martin would read the draft (or, if traveling, have Dora read it to him over the phone). Martin would then rework sections to give them his rhythm and "voice." On top of that, the final pass would happen in real time at the microphone, with Martin using his incredible ability to improvise, re-imagine his own polished text, and even recall and, if it felt right, insert other ways he'd presented the material previously.

Still, at the beginning of the March on Washington speech, Martin's spoken words seemed to hew more closely than either Stanley or I were used to and I shouted a quiet *Hallelujah* when he arrived at the section that referenced the promissory note drawn on the bank of justice that has been returned unpaid due to insufficient funds. I repeated the words in my head as Martin spoke them:

> *It is obvious today that America has defaulted on this promissory note in so far as her citizens of color are concerned. Instead of honoring this sacred obligation, America has given the Negro people a bad check; a check which has come back marked "insufficient funds."*

I didn't truly believe that Martin had not made time to go over the speech carefully, no matter how tired or busy he may have been. Perhaps, after all the years together, I had been lucky enough to tap into his psyche perfectly this one time. If so, perhaps he read the opening material the way I suggested and he actively chose to keep it intact. In her book, *My Life with Martin Luther King, Jr.*, Coretta Scott King recollects the night before The March in their rooms at the Willard: "In our hotel suite Martin began revising his speech."[14] This suggests that he wasn't too busy and instead took time for a careful, late-night review of what I submitted. If that was the case, then this suggested introductory language had passed Martin's extremely high standards.

However, looking more deeply into Mrs. King's description, there also exists the possibility that, understandably, her memory or comprehension of the events surrounding the speech and her marriage to a twentieth-century icon has some extremely personal aspects to it.

There are many scholars, historians, and others who might suggest (and some have) that Martin Luther King, Jr. was such a transcendent writer that he would never require the services of lesser men to draft written material for him. In addition to my direct experience drafting letters, speeches, press statements, and articles for him, history itself strongly suggests that the writing ability of a public figure has little correlation to the amount of writing they actually achieve individually. The factor is time; the higher your profile, the more you need to give your time to the television camera, to the pulpit, to the podium. No matter your talent or your intellect, trusted allies can get rough versions of more projects to your plate than flying solo. Better to take five or six speeches drafted by others and make them your own with judicious and surgical rewriting than to write one speech alone from inception over the same time period, particularly when your Movement is counting on as many speaking engagements as possible to spread the word (as well as to pay the bills). This takes nothing away from Dr. King's ability with a pen. It is simply the hard and fast economics of fame.

Yet fame has another side as well. Fate and hate made Martin a martyr and, in my own lifetime, his memory infused with the kind of unique American mythology usually reserved for the rarest of generals and presidents. Myths, almost by definition, have to stand alone and apart from the common man. People get extremely invested in that mythology. I begrudge no one who sets out to defend Martin Luther King, Jr.'s reputation as a writer and philosopher *sine pari*, but I cannot understand the idea that admitting that the man had people to help him along means something is stripped away. Especially if that means a willful blindness to events as they happened. This does not seem in keeping with Dr. King's legacy and teachings.

In Coretta's book, for example, she leaves out our long meeting in the lobby and my work melding the discussion into a draft in my room. Instead, she focuses on Martin's lone struggle in the hotel suite, explaining that it involved his attempt to condense his speech down to an allotted time. She writes that he'd used a certain analogy two months earlier in

Detroit, but that "in view of the shortness of time given to him, he decided against using that theme. Instead he planned to speak from the theme of America issuing the Negro a bad check, and what this meant in terms of the Emancipation Proclamation, since 1963 was its centenary."[15]

Mrs. King, for whatever reasons, fails to acknowledge that Randolph had already resolved the contentious issue of the time limitation on Martin as the last speaker earlier that day. Yes, her description heightens the last-minute man-against-the-world drama, but, respectfully, her 30,000-feet view does not reflect the facts and circumstances that occurred "on the ground" the day before The March. Consider her reference to the bad check theme. While she carefully says that her husband "planned to speak" about this concept, she never says that he wrote it. The suggestion that Martin was the sole writer is there in her pages, but the definitive statement is not.[16]

Furthermore, in her book Mrs. King suggests that the Detroit analogy Martin felt he did not have enough time for was "his dream of a free united land." Here, she is also hinting that all along Martin had considered the "I Have a Dream" refrain for The March. But though Mrs. King is right in reporting that he'd used that refrain two months earlier at Cobo Hall, I know that on the eve of his speech it was not in his mind to revisit the "Dream."

Because on the Lincoln Memorial steps, Martin, who had made his way into roughly the seventh paragraph of the speech I'd handed in, paused after saying, "We cannot turn back." This alone was nothing unusual. The hesitations and breaks were all part of his oratory process, the rhythms he had mastered at the pulpit. Yet in this split second of silence, something historic and unexpected happened. Into that breach, Mahalia Jackson shouted to him from the speakers and organizers stand. She called out, "Tell 'em about the 'Dream,' Martin, tell 'em about the 'Dream!'" Not many people heard her.

But I did.

And so did Martin.

I would find out years later that Ted Kennedy heard Mahalia as well, but at the time the only person who mattered was the man in front of the microphone. Martin clutched the speaker's podium, a hand on each side, leaned back, and looked at the throng of 250,000 or more assembled in front of the Lincoln Memorial.

I had an instant to wonder what was about to take place. Then I watched Martin push the text of his prepared remarks to one side of the lectern. He shifted gears in a heartbeat, abandoning whatever final version of the balance of the text he'd prepared late the previous night, turning away from whatever notes he'd scrawled in the margins. Observing this from my perch, I knew he'd just put himself in Mahalia's hands, given himself over to the spirit of the moment. That is something a speaker simply cannot know typing away in the quiet hotel suite. It has to be felt right there at the lectern. But by then of course, for most orators, it's too late.

Not for Martin Luther King, Jr., though.

I leaned over and said to the person standing next to me, "These people out there today don't know it yet, but they're about ready to go to church." From his body language and the tone in his voice, I knew Martin was about to transform into the superb Baptist preacher he was; like the three generations of Baptist preachers before him in his family.

Then, honoring Mahalia's request, Martin spoke those words that in retrospect feel destined to ring out that day:

I have a dream . . .

THE MECHANICS OF TRUST

What could possibly motivate a man standing before a crowd of hundreds of thousands, with television cameras beaming his every move to a watching nation and a cluster of microphones tracing his every word, to abandon the prepared text of his speech and begin riffing on a theme that he had used previously without generating much of an enthusiastic reaction?

The answer is twofold: Trust and instinct. Martin's trust was not easily won. Stanley had it, certainly, as did I. Martin was an astute observer of politics, both at the national and the office level. Office politics exists in every organization, from the brutally secular to the charitable and compassionate. The Southern Christian Leadership Conference was no different, and Martin knew that all too well. Those who would discount him as a simple do-gooder or a scholar of only the Bible do a disservice to his powerfully nimble and logical mind. He was quite aware that some of his staff at the SCLC and others he associated with had ambitions and designs. To be clear, these people were truly dedicated to the struggle for freedom. Still, they all wanted his ear, because they all wanted power, praise, promotions, authority, bragging rights, the list goes on. And that affected the way Martin looked at their advice on many important matters. Although they were damaging their own credibility in the very act of trying to strengthen it, for the most part, they couldn't see the unintended consequences.

A scant few, however, really did have Martin's undiluted trust. It was a wonderful thing, a gift not to be taken lightly. The reason that Stanley and I had his devotion was a simple one: We always told him the real score, even if it was hard. He was a powerful figure, and he'd learned that people often had trouble telling truth to power.

Mahalia Jackson also had Martin's trust. She was not just his favorite gospel singer, she was practically his muse. When Martin would get low (and considering all the fronts he was battling on, this wasn't an infrequent situation), he would track Mahalia down wherever she was and call her on the phone. He would say, "I sure could use some cheering up, Mahalia." And she would sing him his favorite hymns. Over the scratchy long-distance phone, without question or complaint. Even if he had just woken her up. She would start singing "Amazing Grace" to Martin a capella, or "The Old Rugged Cross," or "Great Is Thy Faithfulness." And he would close his eyes and lean back in his chair, barely the strength to hold the receiver to his ear, releasing his tension. Letting his uncertainty slip away into the music.

This kind of trust is why Mahalia could shout to him, "Tell 'em about the 'Dream!'" on the steps of the Lincoln Memorial and he would instantly understand the value of the suggestion and run with it.

INSTINCT: THE SPEECH, PART TWO

And so, in an instant, Martin saw the opportunity in front of him. He saw it through Mahalia's eyes. Even, I think, in the midst of deciding its value versus its risk, he had already begun to continue his remarks. And they were beyond the borders of the pages in front of him. But then, Martin was no stranger to extemporaneous speech.

I have often said the sheer processing power of Martin's mind left me awestruck. His dexterity with memory and words ran along the lines of the cut-and-paste function in today's computer programs. The "Letter from a Birmingham Jail" showed his recall for the written material of others; his grueling schedule of speeches illuminated his ability to do the same for his own words. Martin could remember exact phrases from several of his unrelated speeches and discover a new way of linking them together as if they were all parts of a singular, ever-evolving speech. And he could do it on the fly.

Like the finest stage performers, he could live in the moment of his words with his entire being and yet reside in that future tense at the same time, building a bridge ahead of the words, moving everything in the right direction invisibly.

The balance of the speech went on to depart drastically from the metaphor I had set up regarding the promissory note that has not been paid, the effect moving along an up-swinging curve. We started with a solid foundation, but in switching gears, Martin Luther King, Jr. was about to bring a game-changing artistry to the closing of The March.

Any decent public speaker (and certainly any member of the clergy) could have talked succinctly about bad checks and overdue payments for ten or twelve minutes. Roy Wilkins or Cleve Robinson or Ralph Abernathy or A. Philip Randolph would have sufficiently held the crowd's attention with my proposed text. But a different man could not have delivered "I Have a Dream," this meditation on freedom. Naturally, letters spilled across the page cannot even approach re-creating the power of the moment, and it is not the role of this book to tackle the text word by word. In a very real sense, the speech is truly meant to be heard. And though Martin Luther King, Jr. was an astoundingly talented writer, in some ways it would do him a disservice to offer the transcript of the words without the accompanying propulsive force of the voice and mind behind it. It was a performance and has al-ways been judged as such. We are fortunate to live in the Internet Age, and so I encourage every reader of this book to seek out the audio or, better yet, the filmed coverage of the closing speech. You only have to hear Martin speak a handful of these words from his speech and, for the rest of your lifetime, when you read them you will be compelled to hear his signature cadence inside your own skull. And you will marvel at the power his delivery held.

I can hear him now:

> . . . Even though we face the difficulties of today and tomorrow, I still have a dream. It is a dream deeply rooted in the American dream.
>
> I have a dream that one day this nation will rise up and live out the true meaning of its creed: "We hold these truths to be self-evident, that all men are created equal."
>
> I have a dream that one day on the red hills of Georgia, the sons of former slaves and the sons of former slave owners will be able to sit down together at the table of brotherhood.
>
> I have a dream that one day even the state of Mississippi, a state sweltering with the heat of injustice, sweltering with the heat of oppression, will be transformed into an oasis of freedom and justice.
>
> I have a dream that my four little children will one day live in a nation where they will not be judged by the color of their skin but by the content of their character.
>
> I have a dream today!

And on Martin went, building and building upon this handful of deceptively simple words with examples that reflected off each other and yet kept adding another layer of meaning. And he improvised it all. He spoke of children of different races holding hands. He spoke of a great metaphoric leveling of the land and a straightening out of "crooked places," which of course has an amazing dual meaning that would take some writers a lifetime to come up with.

It was hypnotic. Each time Martin told us that he had a dream, the world was pulled one step closer inside it. I'd never seen anything like it.

The crowd was rapt. I was charged with a feverish kind of love for my friend. By the time Martin quoted Samuel Francis Smith's "America" (also known as "My Country 'Tis of Thee") I figured you could measure the tears of joy in the crowd by the gallon. And when he ended with a cried refrain from the spiritual that predated the Emancipation Proclamation, the dizzy sense of history—both past and future—struck me full force:

> *Free at last! Free at last!*
> *Thank God Almighty, we are free at last!*

ELECTRICITY IN THE AIR

So much for providing advance material for The March reporters to feed their editors. I could picture irritable press operators in newspaper pressrooms all over the country prying up their carefully typeset printing plates and starting from scratch.

As Martin went along his improvisational way, people in the crowd had been shouting "Amen," "Preach Dr. King, preach," "Tell it like it is, Dr. King, tell it like it is," offering every version of the encouragements you would hear in a Baptist church multiplied by tens of thousands. The effect was nothing short of soul-stirring.

A shudder went through me as Martin finished. I now knew that I had witnessed something beyond my wildest expectations. In truth, I know it was far beyond Martin's expectations as well. Everyone on the Mall and a whole lot of people watching on their tiny television sets were aware that they had just experienced something transcendent. The "I Have a Dream" speech was less than a minute old, yet it already felt timeless. Martin had reached deep and, with a prod in the right direction from the angelic Mahalia Jackson, come up with a way to paint a portrait of how it felt to be black in America. He had riffed like a masterful jazz soloist. During the second half of his speech, he was like Charlie Parker, John Coltrane, Freddie Hubbard, Sonny Stitt, and Lionel Hampton rolled into one. Martin's words seemed to ignite the spark Mahalia had struck.

During a recent car trip with a friend I was discussing my recollections of The March, and when I told her about Mahalia, she became very excited. She popped the audiobook of

Senator Ted Kennedy's newly released memoir *True Compass* into her CD player and fast-forwarded to the part where Kennedy discusses his memories of the March on Washington. He too had been within earshot of Mahalia when she urged Martin to share his "Dream."

After all these years, I am still sorting out my feelings about the roles of President Kennedy and especially his brother Attorney General Robert Kennedy—complicit participant in Hoover's illegal wiretapping campaign—in our Movement. I long ago ceased being surprised over anything revealed about Robert Kennedy's actions during The March or Martin's lifetime. However, hearing Ted Kennedy's description of The March from his vantage point unleashed emotions in me, even after all this time.

> I had talked to the president about going down for it, but Jack thought that my presence might be counterproductive. I didn't want to be the catalyst that set things off between those who supported the legislation and those who thought it didn't go far enough. Violence was a concern, and Jack advised me to wait and see how things developed.
>
> I still wanted to attend, however, and wrestled with the decision up until August 28th, the day of The March.[17]

I felt satisfied and vindicated as I heard that passage. As the William Cowper hymn goes, "God moves in a mysterious way, His wonders to perform. He plants His footsteps in the sea and rides upon the storm."[18]

"Counterproductive" or not, Ted Kennedy went to the Mall to participate with us. After Martin's speech, Kennedy wrote, "If I hadn't been before, from Grandpa's lessons of discrimination, or from my own awakening to the plight of African-Americans in our nation, I was that day in Washington, D.C., fully baptized into the Civil Rights Movement."[19]

Now almost fifty years after the fact, I finally was able to learn that the effect Martin had on Ted Kennedy on August 28, 1963, was in many ways similar to the one he'd had on me three years prior to The March in the Baptist Church in Baldwin Hills, California. We both had a kind of "conversion" at Martin's hands. What a glorious historic connection between Senator Kennedy and myself. How blessed we both were to share this anointing. Yet how sad I was to learn of this only after Ted Kennedy's death.

Senator, late though it may be, allow me the opportunity to say . . . Welcome to the fold, my brother.

Whenever I am asked to speak to groups, whether they are students, historians, bankers, or religious leaders, the question always comes up: Who today is most like Martin Luther King, Jr.? My answer is always straight out: "No one." And I continue by asking a question of them: "Who today is like Michelangelo, Mozart, Galileo, Shakespeare, or Beethoven?"

I tell with utter conviction to whoever will listen that Martin Luther King, Jr. was *sui generis*—that is, singularly of his own kind. A once-in-a-lifetime (or, more likely, a once-in-a-millennium) figure. And this isn't coming from someone who has made a worship-filled career studying him from afar; I'm speaking as a friend who shared meals and conversation with him. His intellect, his passion, his patience, his faith, his fearlessness—Martin, it sometimes seemed, was not of this Earth.

And the "I Have a Dream" speech was a *sui generis* moment in time. What is most significant about Martin Luther King, Jr.'s appearance at the March on Washington is this: We caught lightning in a bottle because the right man spoke the right words to the right people at the right time. No part of this formula should be undervalued. And though one or two components *could* gel together, the culmination is not likely to be replicated ever again.

Of course, it couldn't have happened with another orator. Martin's choice of words worked as a perfectly balanced outcry of reason and emotion, of anger and hope. His tone of pained indignation in turn matched that note for note. But neither could the "Dream" have happened in another location. We were not simply in the nation's capital but at the foot of the Lincoln Memorial, beneath the nineteen-foot statue of the Great Emancipator. Then into the equation come the hundreds and hundreds of broadcast cameras and microphones blasting Martin's message out into the wide world. What came through to anyone watching or listening was nothing short of a revelation. Martin had a dream, but it was America's wake-up call. Its likes will never come this way again.

And it all played out at just the right moment and in front of a vast freedom-starved crowd right on the edge of its collective patience. We had marched in 1963, the hundredth anniversary of the issuance of the Emancipation Proclamation. Could Abraham Lincoln have imagined that one hundred years after the abolition of slavery, his country would be the kind of place that would make Negroes have to protest for the right to be treated like ordinary citizens?

Even Martin, who would live to speak in front of crowds for nearly another five years, would never again reach these peaks of passion. Some might say his final sermon at the Mason Temple in Memphis, Tennessee, on the evening of April 3, 1968, comes close. But sometimes I wonder if that interpretation is at least partially colored by Martin's assassination the next day. That would be understandable, but it is no way to assess the impact of a speech. There is, of course, real drama to consider in the fact that on the eve of his murder, a man of God would say:

> Like anybody, I would like to live a long life. Longevity has its place. But I'm not concerned about that now. I just want to do God's will. And He's allowed me to go up to the mountain. And I've looked over. And I've seen the Promised Land. I may not get

*there with you. But I want you to know tonight, that we, as a
people, will get to the promised land!*

Given its historical context—Martin's last speech, delivered
just twelve hours before his death on the blood-spattered bal-
cony of Memphis' Lorraine Motel—it is a work that will be
referenced by historians for years to come. It was emotionally
powerful, poignant, and completely extemporaneous. And
although Martin didn't state it directly, it too was a kind of
"Dream"—a look into a possible future for us all ("I've seen
the Promised Land") as well as an almost prescient glimpse
into his own future ("I may not get there with you"). It was
not a speech of inspiration and hope for the coming generations; it was more of a dirge than an anthem. However, it will
always remain a gem, holding a high place in the poetry and
legacy of Martin Luther King, Jr.

But there is only one "I Have a Dream."

It was perhaps five minutes after Martin had finished his
speech that I was able to make my way through the crowd
to him. He was surrounded by a tight ring of people, all
wanting to connect with the person who had moved them
so. Though he was extremely well known before he stepped
up to the lectern, he had stepped down on the other side of
history.

In order to get his attention, I had to grab him tightly by
the arm and yank him toward me. I shouted to be heard over

the buzzing crowd there on the dais, "Martin! Today, you were smokin', just smokin'! Coltrane and Parker rolled into one!"

He gave me his slightly shy smile, but he knew it was true. He felt it. How could you not?

SAVING THE BEST FOR LAST

This was precisely why we had fought so hard to make sure Martin was scheduled as the last speaker on the program. The people had come to see him. Every other speaker that day, dedicated and passionate as they each may have been, was an opening act. Any smart concert promoter will tell you what happens if you put the opening act on *after* the headliner: The audience leaves immediately. They're called openers for a reason. I stood on the Lincoln Memorial steps and watched as the crowd dispersed after "I Have a Dream" and I knew that the reason people were leaving was not because the last speaker had finished. Most, if not nearly all of them, would have done the same thing if Martin had spoken at 2:00 P.M. or even 11:00 A.M. Martin *had* to go last. The world decided it, and the March Committee wisely bent to the will of the people.

There was no sense of rushing, it was more like they dissolved into the evening, but the vast majority of the attendees were gone quickly, casting a surreal quality of quiet over the National Mall.

The next day I visited Washington's best newsstands and collected Wednesday-edition newspapers from all over the East

Coast: *The Boston Globe, The New York Times, The Hartford Courant.* They all ran The March story on their front pages, all above the fold. In *The New York Times,* Russell Baker published an article under the headline "Capital is Occupied by a Gentle Army." That piece, among its other functions, put a stake through the heart of the idea that our mass demonstration was a powder keg just waiting for an open flame:

> No one could remember an invading army quite as gentle as the two hundred thousand Civil Rights marchers who occupied Washington today. . . . The sweetness and patience of the crowd may have set some sort of national high-water mark in mass decency.[20]

As we saw it, the only violence was the sudden jarring shift of perspectives on racial issues we believed we'd inflicted on at least some of our countrymen.

As the week neared its end, papers started arriving from the west and international editions arrived as well. Again, papers from Edinburgh, Mexico City, Rome, Cairo all ran Martin's picture, and many had the complete text of the speech in a big sidebar. The March was covered, of course, but somehow it was all a subset of the speech. When what you've just said is on the front page of every newspaper in the world, you get a pretty good indication that you've made history.

CHAPTER FOUR

A STRIKE OF LIGHTNING, THEN FIFTY YEARS OF ROLLING THUNDER

Dr. King greeting an enthusiastic crowd at the March on Washington.

Photo courtesy National Archives

We have come
over a way that with tears has been watered
We have come
treading our path through the blood of the slaughtered
Out from the gloomy past
till now we stand at last
Where the white gleam
of our bright star is cast

—James Weldon Johnson,
"Lift Every Voice and Sing"

PUTTING A NAME TO IT

There is no rest for the weary. The marchers may have felt relaxed, thinking they were at the end of a long, invigorating day, but we organizers were still on the clock. Directly after the closing hymn, Martin, along with the rest of The March leadership, left for the White House. A caucus on the upcoming Civil Rights Bill had been scheduled, and based on the success of The March, everyone attending from our side felt we were in a position of strength to negotiate. However, when Martin relayed the details to me later, my heart sank. The first thing the president said to Martin was, "I have a dream," but he said it lightly, with a smile. He used the reference as if it were the chorus of a flash-in-the-pan pop song instead of a cry for release from bondage. It appeared Kennedy felt that The March had been "all well and good," but not a rousing success. This came as little surprise to me, but, nevertheless, when Martin told me about the president's attitude it still got under my skin. It was as if we'd just strung a blanket up for a curtain and put on a little show in the barn. Why didn't it impact Kennedy? We assessed the situation. In our political judgment, it accomplished nothing in the way of alleviating the political tension that surrounded the Civil Rights Bill like a cloud. In other words, except for the little pat on the back he might receive in the press for the total absence of violence, The March hadn't done much for *him*.[1]

It seemed as if, in true political fashion, the president was more worried about his party's chances come election day than about the Negroes' chances for justice. Despite the rousing success of The March, he wasn't going to give The Movement any genuine support.

Kennedy's lukewarm view of The March did not stand as an isolated opinion. On the other side of the spectrum, the criticisms mainly focused on what could be perceived as the overly gentle nature of the event. Not enough blood ran in the streets. Some of the more radical members of the civil rights community—Stokely Carmichael and a number of his people within the SNCC, along with some CORE members and even a few labor union leaders—felt disappointed. Interestingly, in Kasher's *The Civil Rights Movement*, he writes, "some Movement stalwarts felt that The March had been manipulated by the president in order to project a prettified image of racial harmony."[2] But does a failed attempt at manipulation really count? This "manipulation" started with the president's trying to bring down the man who gave the "I Have a Dream" speech at The March. It ended with Kennedy personally quoting the instantly famous line directly back to Martin. Neither seemed to have much to do with JFK's honest feelings about the plight of the Negroes. But politics is nothing if not a case study in expediency.

Malcolm X, however, was against The March from the start—not for any supposed government interference but for its policy of inclusion for all races:

> Not long ago, the black man in America was fed a dose of another form of the weakening, lulling and deluding effects of so-called "integration." It was that "Farce on Washington," I call it.[3]

There was one issue on which the dissenters had to agree with the supporters, though. The first words Kennedy had said upon seeing Martin were "I have a dream" for a reason. The wider culture of America had been indoctrinated into the mindset of Martin Luther King, Jr.

The copyright might turn out to be worth the trouble after all.

About a week after The March, I sat in my law office in New York City, filling out the forms that would enable me to officially register Martin's speech with the U.S. Copyright Office. One of my law partners, David Lubell, happened across my open door.

"What are you up to, Clarence?"

I explained to him I was finally getting around to sub-mitting the official copyright paperwork to the Library of Congress on Martin's speech since the handwritten © had merely been an exigency that the law allows for staking a claim on intellectual property without access to the proper forms. The legitimate statutory copyrighting still required the follow-up paperwork.

David looked over my shoulder at the form in the type-writer. "Clarence!" he said, "You can't call it *that*."

I looked at the "Title" line in the middle of the form:

MARTIN LUTHER KING'S

UNPUBLISHED SPEECH OF AUGUST 28TH, 1963

"That's what it is," I told David.

"Maybe so. But what does everybody know it as?"

"'I Have a Dream,'" I answered rote.

"Yeah, 'I Have a Dream.' That's what it's called. So that's what you call it!"

Of course. It had been staring me in the face all week. My "lawyer mind" and my emotional mind were somehow divided, and the man who had felt that electrical blast in the Washington, D.C. air during Martin's speech was not the same man sitting at the desk filling out legal forms.

The author hadn't named it. No one had, officially. Until I submitted the form, it had no name. Yet it had been named nevertheless. It had been named by the world. It had been born and adopted in the same moment.

I inserted the white correction ribbon into the typewriter and cleared the "Title" section. Then I typed in I HAVE A DREAM on the form and signed at the bottom. Within a matter of weeks, it would become the official intellectual property of Martin Luther King, Jr.

At 10:00 A.M. on Sunday, September 15, 1963, the Sixteenth Street Baptist Church was in the midst of its basement Sunday School classes. Outside in the parking lot, a Chevrolet pulled up and a Caucasian man planted a homemade bomb underneath the church steps. The bomb exploded at 10:22, cratering the bottom of the building and showering the parking lot with brick and bits of stained glass. The basement was hit hardest.

When I read about the savage crime in the paper, I looked at my file copy of the registration form from the Copyright Office sitting on my desk. "I Have a Dream." Oh, yeah? They felt like mere words now, words in the ether, drifting away. How could they ever really stand up in the face of guns and knives and bombs? In the face of hatred? We Negroes had wrapped Martin's words around us like a comforting blanket. Comforting, maybe, but obviously not bulletproof.

The afterglow of The March had lasted barely two weeks. The Ku Klux Klan answered Martin's "Dream." The explosion had injured seventeen children. Four young girls attending Christian services had been murdered.

WHY DID "I HAVE A DREAM" CAPTURE THE WORLD?

I have known a few film directors through the years, and I have noticed that no matter what genre or style each specializes in, they all suggest the exact same kind of philosophy when talking about their art. They all view it as a kind of

Birmingham Post-Herald

Alabama's 'Good Morning' Newspaper

HOME EDITION

PRICE FIVE CENTS

VOL. 93—NO. 163   ★   ★   BIRMINGHAM, MONDAY, SEPTEMBER 16, 1963   22 Pages In Two Sections

BOMB BLAST KILLS 4 CHILDREN, INJURES 17 AT CHURCH HERE

Top Federal Officers Help

Justice Dept. To Lead Probe

Troopers Rushed In, Guard Is Alerted

"shared dream." They find nearly intoxicating the ability to directly bring to anyone and everyone the images that are etched in their imagination. Martin's closing speech at The March worked exactly the same way, though he had far fewer tools at his disposal: Only his voice and his choice of words. Film is painstakingly orchestrated with cameras, actors, lights, and music. It mimics life closely and as a result pulls on our emotions. Clearly, it is an art form encumbered by huge logistical challenges, but the results can be fine-tuned to elicit just the right responses from the audience. Public speaking almost never achieves that degree of power. Speeches are often stirring and emotional, but typically they work on the primary level of ideas, not images. Consider Roosevelt's well-known 1933 inaugural speech: "The only thing we have to fear is fear itself." It is stirring, to be sure. But trying to wrap your mind around the concept of "fear" as a verb or even as a noun is an intellectual experience, not an emotional one. And it's certainly not visual. Most speeches are rhetoric, sentence after sentence of bombast that plants ideas in your mind, not images.

The lesson about communication that can be learned from Martin's "I Have a Dream" speech is clear: We are visual creatures, and painting pictures with words can be much more powerful and beneficial than explaining concepts with them.

Like a good film, "I Have a Dream" showed us images of an alternative version of life—a life that *should* be. It clicked together with no missing parts, yet no extraneous ones either. Martin left all the ambiguities out and edited for maximum impact. Picture it now:

> *One day right there in Alabama little black boys and black girls*
> *will be able to join hands with little white boys and white girls*
> *as sisters and brothers.*

The image leaps to the mind immediately. These are not mere words; these are impressions on the retina, plain and simple. The human response upon hearing them is to instantly visualize the tableau, and when listeners do that, they give over a tremendous amount of emotional capital to the speaker. In effect, listeners become invested in the speech.

But then, this verbal imagery wasn't unique to Martin. While it may be rare in political circles, it is an entirely common and acceptable way of stirring the crowd in certain Christian services, notably the Southern Baptist church, which has always been the church for black families in the South. And in the same way that Mahalia Jackson had an organic connection to her audiences, so does the preacher in the Baptist South. That is in part why those discussions in the Willard lobby were so feisty. Those preachers were not just taking a stand; they were taking a grandstand.

So, when I turned to that person beside me and said that those people on the Washington Mall were about to go to church, I didn't necessarily mean it in the sense that a religious sermon was brewing. I didn't know what Martin was going to say. I only knew how he would say it: In the manner of a Baptist preacher. Now, for the vast majority of the people who gathered on the Mall in person, this would not be a real surprise, both because they knew Martin's history and work as a pastor and because they had encountered much the same approach with their church leaders. But we must remember that there were millions of suburban and rural white people tuning in at home. They knew the Martin Luther King, Jr. who had been interviewed on NBC's *Today*. In that well-known 1960 segment, Martin behaves much less like a pastor from Georgia than a level-headed ACLU spokesman.

So for this vast audience, seeing Martin in high dudgeon with his speech was a kind of culture shock. It forced people to listen who never would have listened otherwise. Most of America had never seen him preach. Martin was larger than life on the Lincoln Memorial stage, and he came through the television screen that way too. His words could not be ignored easily because of the presentation and the live audience response. Once those words hit the ears of the listener at home, all that was left was to let their meaning take hold and stir the conscience of everyone who was tuned in.

Not a bad plan to change the country, really. Not bad at all.

BREAKING THE RECORDS

As I mentioned, individuals and businesses had profited from Martin before, but always in fairly indirect ways. The very idea that there were companies that would profit directly from putting Martin's performance of "I Have a Dream" into retail record stores was not something I imagined could happen. But it did, and quickly—within three weeks of the speech. In early September 1963, the words of Martin Luther King, Jr. from the March on Washington were still a topic of conversation around office water coolers and local bars, and to unscrupulous record companies, those people were potential customers. In Harlem, the speech was being broadcast from record stores all across 125th Street. One could buy a copy on nearly every street corner.

Those of us in Martin's inner circle were both flattered and offended by this popularity. As soon as I heard about the record, I knew I had to get a copy. My law offices at the time, with my partners David and Jonathan Lubell, were on lower Broadway, a long way from Harlem. But this was the beginning of Motown artists crossing over outside of the Negro community and connecting with a wider audience. On my way home I came across a record store playing the speech to draw in customers.

It turned out there were two records. Twentieth Century Fox had its newsreel division, Movietone News, film The March. Its recorded music division, Twentieth Century Records, had pulled the sound from the film and released a record of Martin's speech. It was called *Freedom March on Washington August 28, 1963* and even had a picture of Martin on the cover. In addition, the Mister Maestro Record Company had put out its own album entitled *The March on Washington,* a mixture of some of the musical acts sprinkled with ample quotes from "I Have a Dream." Though Mister Maestro showed some restraint by not using Martin's name or likeness on the cover, the packaging looked cheap. I certainly knew Martin had not consented to the distribution of his work in this manner, and I had a feeling that Bob Dylan, Pete Seeger, and the rest hadn't either. Both were unauthorized products, issued by companies that must have assumed that no copyright existed on Martin's work.

In the days before digital piracy cost the music, film, and publishing industries billions of dollars, the one sure thing about copyright protection was that no one out there was policing or enforcing it. It was the job of the violated rights holder, should that person ever discover he or she had been victimized, to alert the authorities. As Martin's lawyer and friend, I had a duty to pursue legal recourse as soon as I got my hands on the records.

I sued on Martin's behalf in federal court to prevent further distribution of the records. It wasn't simply my instinct to protect Martin, nor was it about the finances, though in addition to the suit to enjoin any further sale of the records, I also sued for an accounting of the proceeds from the sales up to that point. At the same time, I was trying to keep us from getting sued: Martin had made a deal with Berry Gordy's Motown Records to issue the only authorized recordings of "I Have a Dream."

Two weeks before Christmas, 1963, I appeared in the Federal Circuit Court in New York. I argued that the defendants were selling Martin's intellectual property without his consent and, of course, without paying anything to him.

The first piece of evidence we presented to make our case was the handwritten © on the press kit copies of the speech. The defense lawyers naturally assumed Martin had waived that statutory right when he spoke in public. Reserving the rights to the speech was the whole reason I had put those symbols on the pages, but it was not enough of an argument to stop the trial then and there.

Many conflicting ideas were batted about in the courtroom: Martin had spoken in a public place, we had distributed copies of the speech beforehand to members of the press, the performance was broadcast live to the entire world. We battled back on all fronts, arguing in our supporting brief that providing the press newsworthy material is substantially different from giving away valuable property, public performance does not equal publication, and these records amounted to theft of Martin's intellectual property.

The defendants' lawyers looked for situations parallel to their clients' positions. They pointed out that *The New York Post* had published the complete text of the speech under the title "I Have a Dream" on September 1, 1963. That was something we knew and approved of, as the *Post* was a news outlet.

What we learned in the courtroom was that the *Post* thereafter offered reprints of the speech for sale. Martin had not consented in any way to such reprinting. Rather than adding to their position that Martin's speech was in the public domain, the defendants succeeded merely in letting us know about another party's infringement of proprietary work for us to consider pursuing.

The significant conclusion reached by the judge was that the copies of the speech were distributed *only to the press,* and this constituted a limited distribution that did not amount to a "publication" sufficient to extinguish Martin's copyright ownership. In his decision, Judge Inzer Bass Wyatt said, "The only reasonable conclusion is that the distribution of copies of the speech was limited to the press. There is not even a suggestion that any copies were offered to, or made available to, the general public."

The court determined that the size of the audience (both in person and the TV and radio audience) did not compromise the copyright. Judge Wyatt wrote the court's opinion:

As an original proposition, it seems unfair and unjust for defendants to use the voice and the words of Dr. King without his consent and for their own financial profit. Of course, [this] decision cannot be made simply because of such a feeling. This is a court of law which must look to legal principles established by the Congress and by higher courts. But under the circumstances here present it does seem that defendants should demonstrate that their use of the voice and words of plaintiff is permitted by legal principles so established. . . .

Ordinarily the public performance of a work—such as delivery of a speech or performance of a play—is not a publication. Thus on general principles there is no reason why Dr. King could not obtain copyright protection. . . .

The substantial argument for defendants, and one which must be carefully considered, is that Dr. King lost any right to copyright protection because what he did in Washington placed the speech in the public domain (dedicated it to the public, as it is sometimes put) because it amounted to a publication without obtaining a copyright. There can be no copyright of any work in the public domain.

The question is: Was this a general publication of the speech so as to place it in the public domain?

The copyright statute itself plainly shows that "oral delivery" of an address is not a dedication to the public. . . . Congress intended copyright protection for "lectures, sermons, addresses" despite such "oral delivery."

It has never been suggested that the number of persons in the audience had any effect on the principle. The "oral delivery" of his speech by Dr. King, no matter how vast his audience, did not amount to a general publication of his literary work.[4]

We had a victory, and though I knew there was financial value in Martin's ownership, my calculations would wind up being off by a decimal place or two.

In the letter I wrote to Dora MacDonald upon sending along the finalized copyright certificates, I noted:

> If "I HAVE A DREAM" is as significant as the press and general public acclaim has indicated, the total value of these rights reserved measured against the potential market for their economic exploitation, is, conservatively, in the thousands of dollars.
>
> Best wishes.
>
> Sincerely,
>
> LUBELL, LUBELL AND JONES
>
> Clarence B. Jones

PRIVILEGED

cbj/pl
encls.

cc: Dr. Martin L. King, Jr.
     Chauncey Eskridge, Esq.
     Edward Clayton

CONFIDENTIAL

K-C 00132

OUT FROM THE GLOOMY PAST

More than forty years later, in the spring of 2005, I was given a wonderful invitation. Stanford University in Palo Alto, California runs one of the world's leading scholarly departments in the field of civil rights study, the Martin Luther King, Jr. Research and Education Institute. In April of that year I was invited to visit as a candidate for the position of the institute's first Scholar in Residence.

It was truly an honor for me. I believe that education is the single most important focus to allow young African Americans to pull themselves out of the traps of poverty, menial work, drugs, and crime. As a result, I felt fortunate to be considered for a position as an educator. I met with the institute's director, Dr. Clayborne Carson. Clay in essence tried to sell me on coming to the institute for my own good. At the time, I had just started work on *What Would Martin Say?* (HarperCollins, 2008), and Clay knew there was no better place to write that particular book than the King Institute, with its wealth of research materials. In the course of going through the features and benefits of the opportunity they were offering, Clay explained the resources of the institute and the breadth and depth of its database. But talk is cheap, he acknowledged. So he asked me to choose a date during those years I worked with Dr. King and he would arrange access to materials from that time for me. I spontaneously offered up the date August 28, 1963, the day of The March. In retrospect, it was perhaps one of the least useful dates for the purposes of Clay's demonstration. The institute might have had more individual pieces of information on that day than nearly any other of King's life, short of the date of his assassination. But it was the day I chose.

It was also an important day in Clay's life, not simply because, without our rally and the "I Have a Dream" speech, there quite possibly might not have ever been a King Institute at Stanford. Clay had been at The March, just in his teens back then. It was his first civil rights demonstration.[5]

One of the staff people in the institute's Research Department went off to retrieve the material. A little while later he brought in a cardboard box with some papers related to that day. Among the documents retrieved from the box was a photocopy of the simple folded program that had been handed out at The March. At the time, neither Dr. Carson nor the institute staff could possibly understand the emotional impact seeing this document had on me. It was the standard March program, except one corner, where it bore a handwritten note to Dr. King—from *me*.

I was looking at a copy of *my own* program from The March, something I'd urgently written on and passed along to Martin. Tears welled up in my eyes as I began to mentally reconstruct the long journey it must have taken from my hand to the King Institute files.

Sometime in the middle of the afternoon on the day of The March someone tapped me on the shoulder. I was standing where I had been for most of the day, on the Lincoln Memorial steps close to the dais. The stranger had seen a man waving for my attention and pointed him out to me. I motioned him over, and the man squeezed his way through the crowd to me. He was a reporter I didn't know (the media credentials hanging on the lanyard around his neck identified him as a representative for the Associated Press), but he had recognized me. He told me that they had just received word on the wire services that Dr. William Edward Burghardt Du Bois, the legendary and eminent Negro historian and scholar, had just died. W. E. B. Du Bois was ninety-five at the time and had been living in Accra, Ghana, after essentially turning his back on the United States. In 1903 he was the man who had tried to tell the world that the "color line" would be the foremost issue in the twentieth century. And he'd been right. Even though Dr. Du Bois was of an advanced age, I found the news shocking. Perhaps it was the coincidence of timing that struck me.

The reporter offered his opinion: "That's a pretty important thing, isn't it?"

I nodded. "Especially today," I said, looking around at the crowd. An intellectual African American icon had fallen. News of Dr. Du Bois' death would be of more importance to these people than almost any other group on Earth I could imagine.

"You should get word to Dr. King," the reporter said. "So they can make an announcement."

It was true; I was in receipt of some information important to The March and the attendees. I looked around for the nearest sheet of paper. It was the copy of the March program I was holding in my hand.

I clicked my ballpoint pen and wrote:

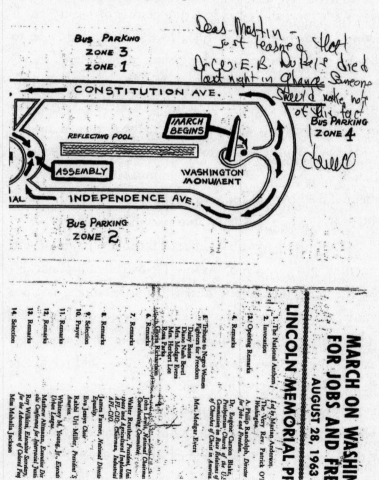

I folded the program lengthwise with my note facing in so it could not be read casually. Then I asked the man in front of me, a stranger in the crowd, to pass it along. "To Martin Luther King," I said. He nodded and tapped the person next to him on the shoulder. "This is for Dr. King," I heard him say. With voice and a hand-waving gesture that said "Pass it along," I watched the note make its way closer and closer to Martin. By a chain of nameless people at The March standing between the dais and me, my note was passed from person to person, unopened, until it was handed to Martin. He opened and read it, then stood up halfway, turned around and waved to me with a sorrowful expression, acknowledging that he'd received it. Within a few minutes Roy Wilkins, president of the NAACP, approached the lectern and announced W. E. B. Du Bois' passing to the assembled crowd.

Presumably Martin had placed the folded program with my note into a pocket of his suit. He had a habit of pocketing the things throughout the day that he felt might have potential lasting importance. At day's end he would lay these items out on his bureau—perhaps ten or twelve business cards, notes, phone numbers, and the like—and reevaluate them. Most would be discarded. A few he would keep.

After The March, he must have done the same thing. He likely passed along the items he wanted to keep to Coretta. She kept these personal items in several boxes in their basement, along with other treasures, including handwritten copies of some of Martin's sermons.

After his death, Coretta donated many of the materials to various scholarly organizations. A photocopy of my hand-written note on the program of The March was turned over to Dr. Carson and the institute, filed as part of relevant King material from that date. It made its way from my hand to Martin's, then made its way through all these years and across this great country back into my hand.

I stood there, feeling the biochemical cocktail racing through my blood, forcing me to run the emotional spectrum from love to loss and hitting every sharp feeling in between. I was thunderstruck.

I looked at the copy of the program in my hand. This was more than instruction on the way history echoes back to us. I felt Martin King, my friend, reaching out and saying to me, "Clarence, keep our 'Dream' alive."

CHAPTER FIVE

IN THE PRESENT, TENSE

Dr. King, Whitney Young, and James Farmer visit with President Johnson in the Oval Office.

Photo courtesy National Archives

You do not take a person who, for years, has been hobbled by chains and liberate him, bring him up to the starting line of a race and then say, "You are free to compete with all the others," and still justly believe that you have been completely fair.

—President Lyndon B. Johnson,
Howard University
Commencement Speech,
June 1965

WELCOME TO FUNTOWN

Ideas are the change agents of our world, and words are the building blocks of those ideas. Their DNA. In effect, I believe not only that words can change destinies but that they are the fundamental path to do so. Not fists, guns, tanks, or bombs. *Words*.

The trick, of course, is getting people to listen. The first step is to find a way to allow them to hear. They *are* two different things, hearing and listening. That Friday evening in my California home in February 1960, when Martin made his plea—The Movement had lots of white lawyers offering to assist them, and he was grateful, but he wanted to encourage "young Negro lawyers" like me to also help—I *listened* to him. Two days later, at the Baptist church in Baldwin Hills, I *heard* him.

A man shouting at the top of his lungs seems to be whispering from a hundred feet away, silent from a thousand. In order to be heard, having a platform is crucial.[1] Martin had the world's biggest platform, the March on Washington. Five hundred news cameras were pointed at him at that time—more in one place than ever in the history of media. People were undoubtedly listening. But did they *hear*?

That question can be answered by taking a look at the American sociopolitical landscape from our vantage point nearly fifty years later. Because, for all its hopeful attributes, the "I Have a Dream" speech is really a call to action. It was designed, even in improvisation, to make people take a hands-on approach to transforming its vision into daily reality. Martin had a dream the same way an architect has a blueprint. Neither one is actually a part of the fabric of the world when it is made, but both can turn into something so substantial they cannot be ignored, erased, or toppled.

In December 2008, I traveled to Paris as the guest of the French organization SOS Racisme and the mayor of Paris, Bertrand Delanoë. My invitation was part of Paris' celebration of the sixtieth anniversary of the United Nations' Declaration of Human Rights, the ninth World Summit of Nobel Peace laureates, and commemoration of the legacy of Dr. King, forty years after his death.

Nobel laureates such as F. W. de Klerk of South Africa, Ingrid Betancourt, Lech Walesa, John Hume, Betty Williams, and the renowned rock star Bono were there, along with many other luminaries from all over the world.[2] During the conference the questions asked of me again and again were: *Is Barack Obama another Martin Luther King, Jr.? What would Dr. King say about the election of Obama? Does the election of Obama as the first African American president of the United States mean that Dr. King's dream has been fulfilled?*

Clearly, the question of whether Martin's "Dream" has been realized in the twenty-first century is one that is the subject of discussion and consideration beyond the borders of the United States. These inquiries are of a piece, and they indicate that the fundamental question to answer is simply this: In the nearly half a century since Martin Luther King, Jr., had his dream, has it come true?

This is posed as a yes-or-no question, and would have been unthinkably naive in the years after the March on Washington but before the Barack Obama presidency. The answer pre-election night 2008 would, of course, have been a resounding no. Post-election night, the issue becomes cloudier. Those who argue that our election of an African American president proves that racism is a thing of the past are not looking closely at the subtleties of racism. Of course progress has been made toward respect for African Americans, and Barack Obama is living proof of that, but consider the virulent hatred that bubbled up as Obama gained momentum in the primaries—the unsettling Halloween costumes and email-forwarded jokes.

In the midst of the 2008 primaries, I had a conversation with an elderly African American woman in Oakland. She explained why she was going to vote for Hillary Clinton instead of Barack Obama. She told me she really wanted to vote for Obama but she felt like a grandmother towards him and, as such, felt a moral obligation to protect him. If she voted for him for president and he got elected, she suggested, "They will do to him what they did to President Kennedy and Dr. King." The fact that we were dealing with the "I don't want him to win for *his* sake, because I just know he's going to be assassinated" trope comes as no surprise, but still—is that the voice of a color-blind nation?

Even Obama's eventual running mate and vice president, Joe Biden, was scrutinized by the media over a possibly racist comment. Among a string of adjectives he used to describe his then-opponent Obama, Biden offered "African American" and then the word "clean." It caused a public relations problem on Biden's first day of campaigning for the presidency. And while he kept backpedaling, saying he meant the phrase to invoke the idea there were no skeletons in Obama's closet, one cannot help but wonder about that. Would Biden or any other privileged public servant ever describe someone like John Kerry as "white and clean"? It is doubtful.[3]

And that's the people *on* the team. What should be of more concern, grave concern actually, is the rising antipathy, sheer meanness, disrespect, anger, and hostility not just toward President Obama's policies but to the man personally, as well as the First Lady. People in a position to know, in contact with the White House, have shared information with me that First Lady Michelle Obama has received more threats to her personal safety than all other previous first ladies *combined*.

Where is all of this hatred and escalating hostility toward the president coming from? It's hard to pinpoint, but it seems to transcend traditional policy and party differences.

So, where is the post-racial America it has been suggested we have achieved, proven by the election of Barack Obama? Nowhere in sight. It is an understatement to point out that the election of an African American president does not mean a society wholly accepting of all African Americans. Racism continues to fester in every city, town, and village of this country. So even in a post-Obama era, we can safely (if somewhat sadly) say that we have not fully achieved the "Dream." But the issue should not really be framed as a yes-or-no question, because the situation is one of degrees. The problems of racial prejudice exist on a continuum. A better question might be: Have we even come close?

An accurate answer to this question requires a look at the underlying political principles and ideology that powered the philosophical engine of Martin Luther King, Jr., not just in this one speech but within ideas he spent his entire adult lifetime considering. Admittedly, I may have an advantage in reviewing his "Dream" because I can relate it not only to his other speeches but also to my real-life experiences with the man. This allows me to round out the tenets that framed his speech in a way most historians cannot.

The "Dream" was not an ethereal idea; it was grounded. In fact, though that section of Martin's speech was improvised, he had explored much of the same territory in his transcendent "Letter from a Birmingham Jail." A vision of a vastly different future for his children was always in the forefront of Martin's mind. Part of why the speech at the

March on Washington is so revered is because it clearly feels like a capstone to his constant consideration of what the country would be like for the next generation of Negroes. In the "Letter," Martin forces readers to put themselves in the place of every Negro parent, trying to get them to imagine how they would feel explaining to their child why they were denied entrance to an exciting amusement park:

> Your tongue twisted and your speech stammering as you seek to explain to your six-year-old daughter why she can't go to the public amusement park that has just been advertised on television, and see tears welling up in her eyes when she is told that Funtown is closed to colored children, and see ominous clouds of inferiority beginning to form in her little mental sky, and see her beginning to distort her personality by developing an unconscious bitterness toward white people; when you have to concoct an answer for a five-year-old son who is asking: "Daddy, why do white people treat colored people so mean?"

Martin spent much of his short life thinking about his children and whether he could do something to prevent them from enduring the same experiences with white racism he had gone through. Remember, he did not dream of a better life for Negroes without historical context. The "essence" of his dream for African Americans ten, twenty, forty, or more years after the March on Washington was this: A United

States of America where every American man, woman, and child has the equal opportunity—educationally, economically, culturally, and politically—to participate in our society and develop themselves to the maximum of their abilities, irrespective of the color of their skin or ethnicity.

What does the concept of equal opportunity to participate in society to the maximum of one's potential without regard to race or ethnicity assume? It assumes that, all other things being equal, African Americans should have access to the same opportunities that whites and other groups have in our country. But that's been the problem; this "all other things being equal" is the 800-pound gorilla in the room of race relations in America. Because our country has not truly leveled the playing field at all. The Thirteenth, Fourteenth, and Fifteenth Amendments along with various civil rights bills and Supreme Court decisions aimed at dismantling racial segregation in public education, interstate and intrastate transportation, and racially restrictive covenants in rental housing have not constituted or created "all other things being equal." The Supreme Court decision in *Baker v. Carr* clarified the "one person, one vote" issue. But the Voting Rights Act of 1965 remains, after the Emancipation Proclamation, the Brown decision of 1954, and the Civil Rights Acts of 1957 and 1964, the single most important event to date that enables Dr. King's dream the chance at becoming realized.

Full realization of the dream will require addressing the oppressive inequality of income and wealth in America.

This is a capitalist society, and each individual's market power is key to how he is treated. There remains an enormous division between the races when it comes to median income, home ownership, education, life expectancy, the incarceration rate, drug use, and death rate.[4]

The issue at the heart of all these problems is the idea that freedom and economic opportunity are interchangeable; that freedom *is* economic opportunity. This is false logic. Freedom without economic opportunity is in fact just a variant form of oppression. Further, this thinking is dangerous to the African American community because it obscures the definitive criterion necessary in evaluating the realization of Martin's "Dream" for African Americans in the twenty-first century and beyond: Wealth.

MONEY MAKES THE WORLD GO 'ROUND

In the autumn of 2011, the "Occupy Wall Street" protest began. As I write, the demonstrations are ongoing and spreading from city to city. There have been some rumors of police brutality, there have been arrests, and there has been careful assessment on what actions should be taken by local authorities who know they're in the media spotlight. Overall, the movement's impact won't be sorted out for some time.

Some of the post-King Civil Rights leadership wants to identify this form of protest as an extension of the Civil

Rights Movement. It is not. I know that without the legacy of Dr. King, these groups of concerned Americans would likely have no blueprint to follow in creating a large-scale and media-savvy protest. And Occupy Wall Street may well be the most innovative movement for social and economic justice since Dr. King. But it is qualitatively different. It is raising questions that go to the very foundation and *raison d'être* of our economic system: Capitalism. Civil Rights protests were—and are—about a system of laws, policies, and social standards that treated particular groups of people with inequality. This new movement asserts that the underpinnings of the world economy are corrupt to their core, and work against the interests of all but a few of us. The difference, in other words: The Civil Rights Movement demanded fair play in the game; the Occupy Wall Street movement suggests the whole game is rigged to begin with. Its focus is highlighting the Obama administration's apparent double standard in handling the problems of the financial markets in relation to his approach to solving the problems of American families.

Some media pundits call the Occupy Wall Street people "socialist." Some categorize them as people "on the dole" who have never wanted or tried to get a job. Occupy Wall Street is America's own version of the Arab Spring. They are the moral and ideological children of the legacy of Martin Luther King, Jr. As such, they carry a great responsibility to assure that their movement remains nonviolent. They must oppose those forces that would seek to "hijack" their grievances based on an antithetical agenda of nihilistic violence or who seek to wrap themselves in the imprimatur of the authenticity of their movement.

Dr. King would have been among the first to publicly support Occupy Wall Street. He would not have waited to gauge public opinion as to whether it was "politically" right or appropriate to embrace and support its objectives.

Various labor leaders, religious leaders, and even some leaders of the Democratic Party are joining and participating in Occupy Wall Street. The movement seems to be connecting the dots on certain fundamental issues of poverty, income inequality, and economic injustice—issues that, for those inside the Civil Rights Movement, have always been clearly tied together. Generally speaking, families that are financially disadvantaged remain in the vacuum of poverty from one generation to the next. While there are exceptions, they do prove the rule. The single most important historical handicap to full realization of Martin's "Dream" remains the absence of capital or economic reparations for our ancestors whom Lincoln set "free" with his Emancipation Proclamation of 1863. The Thirty-ninth Congress, which enacted Reconstruction legislation following the Civil War, was well aware of the economic deficit that newly freed slaves (and their children, their grandchildren, their great-grandchildren, etc.) would have in developing the maximum of their potential in years to come.

One of the most important capital assets then, as now, was land. Land ownership combined with a means of economic production meant a family could prosper. For this reason, the government intended to grant forty acres and a mule to every emancipated slave to enable him to have a base of capital and means of production to sustain his family and to gain an economic foothold for future generations. The failure of the Reconstruction Congress and subsequent Congresses to honor this commitment meant there was no capital asset that could be transferred from generation to generation, with the possibility of gathering value, within the African American family.

In July 1967, President Lyndon B. Johnson empanelled a commission led by Illinois governor Otto Kerner. There had been a series of race riots across the country—Detroit, Newark, Chicago, and other major cities—and the president wanted answers on what caused them and how to stop them. Early in 1968, after seven months of study, the Kerner Commission issued its findings on racial relations in America. The conclusion of the Kerner Commission Report was boiled down to fourteen pointed words, a painful headline:

OUR NATION IS MOVING
TOWARD TWO SOCIETIES
ONE BLACK, ONE WHITE—
SEPARATE AND UNEQUAL[5]

Martin could have told President Johnson the same thing without all the fuss of creating a commission. In fact, he did.

The intervening thirty years did little to change the climate, according to the 1997 report from the Milton S. Eisenhower Foundation, which concluded that "The rich are getting richer, the poor and working class are getting poorer, and minorities are suffering disproportionately."[6] And at the root of all this is the disparity of capital across racial lines. Remember, it's not about wages and it's not about work. It's about financial structure and the almost unbelievable power of compound interest, the concept that money makes money. It's about the economic tools whites reserved for themselves even as they decided Negroes were human beings after all.

The contemporary reaction among most white people whenever the issue of reparations is raised is something like, "Hey, I wasn't there, I didn't do anything to harm the ancestors of the current generation of African Americans. So I have no financial or moral responsibility for the subsequent absence of capital, land, or other economic assets which this generation of African Americans could have inherited."

That may be technically true, but by focusing on individual decision making, this argument misses the point that there is an underlying reason our racial problems will not simply go away through antidiscrimination laws. If you take over your friend's place as the banker in the middle of a game of Monopoly, it may not be your fault if your opponent tells you the game started without him getting any money, but you're still stuck with the fact that there is no way for him to win. Looking at it from that angle, it's amazing that anyone in the opponent's position would even *try* to play by the rules.

Even in his earliest speeches, Martin raised the issue of reparations for Negroes to redress the adverse economic consequences of slavery and institutionalized racism upon subsequent generations. Consider this 1965 address he gave in San Francisco:

> *In 1863 the Negro was granted freedom from chattel slavery through the Emancipation Proclamation. He wasn't given any land to make that freedom meaningful.*
>
> *You know that was almost like having a man in jail for thirty to forty years and pretty soon you discover that he has been falsely charged. He is innocent of the charge he was convicted of. Then, you come up to him saying [on the day of his release] "We see that you are not guilty, so you are now free;" at the same time, you refuse to give him any bus fare to get to town. You refuse to give him any money to buy clothes, any money to get on his feet again.*
>
> *This is exactly what happened to the Black man. He was told he was free but he was penniless. He was illiterate, standing around not knowing where to go or what to do. [7]*

Martin, Stanley, and I often discussed, at least philosophically, how deeply committed he was to reparations as a form of equity parity for Negroes. Martin Luther King, Jr., was not a money-oriented man, and his philosophy regarding reparations was not strictly a financial demand.[8] Rather, he used the discussion of money to train the spotlight of attention on the fact that purposeful decisions by the government of a capitalist society created an underclass in a very simple way—abolition may have let the Negro go, but it did not free him.

We wrestled with ways to frame the issue that would have the broadest appeal to most Americans, white and black. Martin's logic was made clear in a 1965 interview that appeared in *Playboy* magazine:

> Can any fair-minded citizen deny that the Negro has been deprived? Few people reflect that for two centuries the Negro was enslaved and robbed of *any* wages—potential accrued wealth which would have been the legacy of his descendants. *All* of America's wealth today could not adequately compensate its Negroes for his centuries of exploitation and humiliation. It is an economic fact that a program such as I propose would certainly cost far less than any computation of two centuries of unpaid wages plus accumulated interest. In any case, I do not intend that this program of economic aid should only go to the Negro; it should benefit the disadvantaged of all races. [9]

The word "reparations" was used only occasionally in discussions with Martin. However, the concept was often discussed in the form of a "Bill of Rights for the Disadvantaged" or "Guaranteed Income." Whatever phrases were used, however, his ideas and proposals aimed at addressing the economic and social consequences of slavery always included references to disadvantaged poor white people as well as Negroes. Over the many years following this interview, it has become clear that one of the principal beneficiaries of the reparations concept and affirmative action have been middle-class white women.[10]

In speaking about a proposed "Bill of Rights for the Disadvantaged," Martin said:

> *While Negroes form the vast majority of America's disadvantaged, there are millions of white poor who would also benefit from such a bill. The moral justifications for special measures for Negroes are rooted in the robberies inherent in the institution of slavery. As long as labor was cheapened by the involuntary servitude of the black man, the freedom of white labor, especially in the South, was little more than a myth. It was free only to bargain from the depressed base imposed by slavery upon the whole labor market. Nor did this derivative bondage end when formal slavery gave way to the de facto slavery of discrimination.* [11]

This historical lack of economic parity poses the greatest obstacle to African Americans taking full advantage of whatever opportunity might be equally available to them to fully develop their God-given potential in a post-"I Have a Dream"

America. Martin's "Dream" will not be realized today, to-morrow, or in the foreseeable future unless and until the historical economic disparity between comparable generations of white and African Americans is substantially reduced or eliminated.

President Johnson understood this, and in spite of the far-reaching political and social justice laws enacted during his presidency, he also knew it wasn't enough. In a commencement speech at Howard University in 1965 he said:

> The Voting Rights Bill will be the latest, and among the most important, in a long series of victories. But this victory—as Winston Churchill said of another triumph for freedom—"is not the end. It is not even the beginning of the end. But it is, perhaps, the end of the beginning."

Later in his address, Johnson acknowledged that many whites inherited poverty as well, but he added that for the African Americans:

> There is a second cause—much more difficult to explain, more deeply grounded, more desperate in its force. It is the devastating heritage of long years of slavery; and a century of oppression, hatred, and injustice.
>
> For Negro poverty is not white poverty. Many of its causes and many of its cures are the same. But there are differences—deep, corrosive, obstinate differences—radiating painful roots

into the community, and into the family, and the nature of the individual.

> *These differences are not racial differences. They are solely and simply the consequence of ancient brutality, past injustice, and present prejudice. They are anguishing to observe. For the Negro they are a constant reminder of oppression.*

The speech is filled with nods to the idea of reparations. But the key to remember here is that this was a *sitting president* speaking, anguished over the unfairness of the situation without the ideas or the power to do anything about it.[12]

That said, I am a realist. I can think of no economic process that could possibly account for reparations in any manner that would ever be approved by any but the tiniest sliver of liberal white voters. Moreover, the realpolitik demonstrated in the 2010 midterm elections, where the Republicans and the Tea Party assaulted the Democrats' base of power, confirmed that any serious national discussion of the absence of economic parity for today's African Americans as a result of the consequences of slavery will be tabled for the near future at a minimum. Current issues overshadowing any such discourse include illegal immigration, high unemployment, housing foreclosures, the legitimacy of continuing the war in Afghanistan, our exorbitant national debt, the growing public perception of financial unfairness between the bank bail-outs and the assistance for millions of financially stressed Americans, and the tight credit market for small business despite the nearly three trillion of cash reserves made possible by taxpayers' funding of the Troubled Asset Relief Program, or (formerly "toxic" until the White House communication consultants saw how that message was registering with the public).

It may be that the qualitative changes in our domestic economy—the unprecedented, ubiquitous impact of technology linked to financial engineering that centers on the creation of wealth and new forms of capital assets—will make the failure of reparations following slavery forever beyond practical federally mandated redress for current and future generations of post-"Dream" African Americans.

Slavery and the subsequent abandonment of the congressional grant of forty acres and a mule stunted the growth of potential fruit on the economic family tree of generations of African Americans. The fact that the reinvigoration and repair of those roots may be beyond our current society's capacity to redress does not mean that the tree can't be watered and the branches can't be strengthened to enable more abundant and fuller fruit to grow. Nor does it mean that the Obama Administration and future administrations get "off the hook," absolved of any moral responsibility for remaining concerned about effective ways to practically achieve what the 39th Congress attempted and Lyndon Johnson subsequently tried to do.

Interestingly, in Martin's April 4, 1967, public opposition to the Vietnam War, he warned President Johnson that

the war's continuation was squandering precious financial resources needed to address critical domestic economic problems
of our nation, including Johnson's ability to redress the absence
of economic parity for African Americans. President Obama
should be commended for honoring his campaign pledge to
end the war in Iraq. Only the "neocons" and those political
pundits who can't find a war they don't like oppose his decision
to bring all our troops home from Iraq by the end of 2011.
Those questioning the wisdom and cost of the continued war
in Afghanistan are saying substantially the same thing Martin
said about the financial effects of the Vietnam War. If the history repeats, so do the problems associated with that history.

This may be *the defining challenge* confronting Martin's
post-"Dream" America in the twenty-first century.

THE SHEPHERDLESS FLOCK

As it has been for most of the previous century, current culture in America is largely a by-product of today's "Black Experience" and of the legacy of slavery and segregation,
adopted by the mainstream—whether it is in language,
dance, fashion, sports, or music. Is this more cultural theft by
the white man, as some African American artists insist, or is
it a joining of two worlds and a sign of respect? I prefer to
think the latter, although it often seems that cutting-edge en-
deavors in the African American community—from blues
licks, to dance moves, to clothing styles—are appropriated
precisely when the time is right to profit.

In a certain sense, it may be that many white Americans see African Americans as heroic. The Black Experience seems to go right to the edge and take another step past, an inadvertent avant garde for others eager to be cool but unwilling to stake out the territory themselves. When I reflect on this, I think of Eldridge Cleaver's searing passage:

> The white youth of today have begun to react to the fact that the "American Way of Life" is a fossil of history. What do they care if their old baldheaded and crew-cut elders don't dig their caveman mops? They couldn't care less about the old, stiffassed honkies who don't like their new dances: Frug, Monkey, Jerk, Swim, Watusi. All they know is that it feels good to swing to way-out body-rhythms instead of dragassing across the dance floor like zombies to the dead beat of mind-smothered Mickey Mouse music. [13]

The goal might well be to find the next frontier when the last one loses its luster after getting mainstreamed.

Yes, there seems to be something of a community trait here. As a group, we are all about searching out the next new thing. But sometimes the hottest thing today is a take on something old school. Something retro, brought back with a twist.

I haven't seen it happen yet, but I'm hopeful that the ideologies of the old Civil Rights Movement—its passions, its compassions, its strategies—will come back into style, ride a revival wave. Call it the "New Movement." There is still plenty to protest about.

No, I haven't seen it *quite* yet, though there is change in the air.

Sadly, those with less compassionate agendas for America seem better equipped to see the vacuum of power and fill it. On August 28, 2010, forty-seven years to the day after the March on Washington, radio and Fox News television talk show host Glenn Beck held a rally to "Restore America's Honor" at the Lincoln Memorial site. It was billed as a non-political event but I saw it clearly as political theater—an attempt to further invigorate the far-right Republican "Tea Party" base through an evangelical call. Many people working on the modern civil rights front viewed this rally as a fundamentalist, conservative, and yes, white co-opting of the iconic moment in the black struggle. And as a result, many took offense. But I wasn't one of them.

The historical perception of us-against-them, a general white resistance (or, at least, indifference) to the struggle for African American equality is largely a fallacy in my experience.

For one thing, nearly a quarter of the people who showed up to our 1963 March were white. That wasn't an aberration. Throughout the sixties I spent a lot of time in the living rooms of many white families who were eager to offer both their time and financial support to the cause. One of

Dr. King's most important intellectual contributions to the Civil Rights Movement was his thesis that as long as African Americans represented only 10 to 12 percent of the population, we could not hope to change the country unless we convinced a significant portion of the majority that it was in their self-interest to help us do so.

And so we wanted, encouraged, and prayed for "white America" to take an active interest in our goals. But somewhere along the way, it seems that particular part of our message has gotten lost. For a number of years there has been a strong black backlash against various "establishment" factions that have embraced Martin Luther King, Jr.'s legacy from the March on Washington. If, in fact, the goal is for us all to get along in a post-racial country, why shouldn't something like Beck's rally, a peaceful airing of political grievances and desired changes, be commended? Because in the view of some genuine, earnest, and liberal-minded people, white people invoking Dr. King's vision is tantamount to stealing.

In answer to this perceived violation, Reverend Al Sharpton, who suggested to CBS News that Beck was making "a blatant attempt to hijack a movement that changed America," organized a gathering away from the Mall at D.C.'s Dunbar High School—a countermarch to "reclaim the 'Dream.'"

In the online commentary my coauthor and I wrote for *The Huffington Post* on the anniversary's Beck-versus-Sharpton aftermath, we tried to look at this all from Martin's perspective. With respect to the Glenn Beck rally:

All these years after the "I Have a Dream" speech, on its anniversary, every time King's name was spoken or the "Dream" was referenced, the crowd, predominantly white, cheered. Many of whom, it is fair to imagine, are the descendents of those whites who opposed equality and, yes, "honor" for African Americans a half century earlier.

. . . In 1963, only 20–25% of the attendees were white; last weekend, 80–90% of the estimated Beck participants were white. And it's worth saying again: They applauded Dr. King's legacy at every turn.

And with respect to Sharpton's criticism of the Beck rally at the time, we wrote:

In trying to take ownership or view Beck's invocation of King as some kind of theft, members of the modern black struggle are turning off potential allies and, more importantly, missing the point that Dr. King's "Dream" was an American dream, not just an African American dream.

Since then, I've been pleased to see the political maturity of my friend Reverend Sharpton articulated on his new MSNBC show.

Rather than view the event as a hijacking, Glenn Beck's gathering can perhaps be more instructive by viewing it as a litmus test. To date, no matter which crowd estimates you believe, the rally was clearly the largest organized expression of dissatisfaction with the presidency of Barack Obama. The

Republicans strong gains in the 2010 midterm elections (and even more spectacularly, Republican Scott Brown's taking, in the special election following Ted Kennedy's death, of the Massachusetts senatorial seat that had been occupied by Democrats for nearly sixty consecutive years) was due to the Republican Party's strategic, relentless focus on voter dissatisfaction with the nation's economy and connecting it with an alleged failure of Obama's leadership during this time of real crisis.

President Obama and his advisors decided to spend most of his post-election political capital in reforming healthcare. Initially, I had been critical of this chosen priority against the background of rising unemployment and house foreclosures. It appeared to undermine the credibility of the first half of his presidency and revealed the great disparity between the level of expectations for change that Candidate Obama told us we could believe in and the absence of such change in the lives of average Americans. Upon further reflection, I began to speculate on the pledge and moral commitment Candidate Obama may have made to Senator Ted Kennedy and his family (following the senator's death on August 25, 2009) to make healthcare more affordable and accessible. Accordingly, the president may have earned a little "slack" for his decision to invest his political capital in healthcare during his first year in office.

Nevertheless, in contrast with the aggressive, politically preemptive "take no prisoners" leadership initiatives of his campaign, Obama as president for most of his first term seems to have let his opposition define who he is and what he stands for. Without forcefully mounting any political counterattack against, for example, claims that he is not really an American citizen, but a Muslim Kenyan national "illegally" and "illegitimately" occupying the White House, Obama is, in essence, allowing easily swayed citizens to believe such nonsense.

Taking the high road doesn't work in politics anymore, if indeed it ever did.

In May 1963, I had a contentious meeting with Robert Kennedy.[14] In defending the civil rights achievements of his brother John and the Justice Department during his tenure as attorney general of the United States, RFK predicated that "in forty years" a Negro might be president of the United States.

This was no small surprise to hear coming from the man who had been convinced, due to The Movement's alleged potential danger, of all things, to sign wiretap authorizations on Stanley, Martin, and me. Those of us who worked closely with Martin never contemplated the realistic possibility of a black president of the United States in any of our lifetimes. Robert Kennedy turned out to be off by only five years, though of course he would never live to see it.

As I wrote in an op-ed piece for CNN.com on the eve of Barack Obama's inauguration, after the assassination of

President John F. Kennedy, most of us advising Martin concluded that no fundamental change in race relations in America could be accomplished and successfully sustained unless it was done under the political leadership of a white man from the South. Major historic civil rights legislation under Texan president Johnson was followed by the presidencies of other white southern political leaders. Jimmy Carter (Georgia), Bill Clinton (Arkansas), and George W. Bush (Texas) all seemed to validate our original political thesis. Our belief was predicated on the political analysis that assumed America would be more willing to follow a *white southern* political leader on the issue of race relations and equal economic opportunity than a politician from any other part of our country. But the 2008 Democratic Primary to determine the presidential nominee seemed to skip several steps in the evolution of equality by pitting an African American candidate against a female one. Both were serious contenders. My coauthor and I were together during the Super Tuesday primary. We watched in awe as former First Lady Hillary Rodham Clinton battled Barack Obama. Representatives of two groups that had previously been denied the vote were squaring off in a bid for the highest office in the land. It was not a perfect night at the polls for Obama, but it was historic nonetheless. Stuart asked me if I ever thought I would live to see the day this would be happening for an African American. My answer was no. At the time, I thought it was probably possible that someday America might elect an African American as president, but not in my lifetime. I am pleased that my countrymen had a more optimistic view of our electorate than I.

President Obama represents a new generation in the twenty-first century that has developed its own unique genre of political leadership. A November 2008 story in *Business Week* described him as "A Leader for the 'We Generation'" and suggested "The sweeping victory of Barack Obama ushers in a new era of leadership that will affect every aspect of American institutions and that sounds a death knell for the top-down, power-oriented leadership prevalent in the 20th century."[15] That felt true at the time. In 2008, Candidate Obama, like Martin Luther King, Jr. before him, articulated a prophetic hope and optimism about the goodness of our people—irrespective of race, color, or gender. But as Obama gears up for the 2012 campaign, it seems that the country's economic troubles, hand-in-hand with the right's PR assault aimed at defeating his re-election at all costs, have soured that perception of optimism. President Obama is accused of proposing job recovery and deficit reduction programs that are based on "class warfare." Some on the left, part of Obama's most enthusiastic original voter base, feel "betrayed," particularly with respect to the decisions regarding the financial bailout programs.

Today's realization of Martin's "Dream" is partially dependent on the extent to which the current generation of

African American leaders play a constructive role under the political dynamic of an African American in the White House. Obama's election has sparked a debate among people such as Reverend Al Sharpton, media personalities Tavis Smiley and Tom Joyner, Professors Michael Eric Dyson and Cornel West, Marc Morial (president of the NUL), Benjamin Jealous (president of the NAACP), and other such leaders as to whether he, as president of *all* people in the United States, nevertheless should be especially responsive to what is generically described as a "Black Agenda." In early 2010, following the Obama administration's strenuous efforts to enact a major health reform bill and with the continued high joblessness within the African American community, discussion of this issue became particularly intense and even at times acrimonious. The assumption is that such an agenda requires special and unique attention and action by President Obama separate, above, and beyond his oath to represent everyone in our country. I believe such a debate has limited productive value, if any at all. The benchmark should be whether the Obama Administration addresses those issues that specifically impact African Americans relative to other, non-central issues. To the extent that the comparison is favorable and those issues are inextricably tied to realizing Martin's "Dream," current black leadership should applaud and support those efforts, as they should when a white president behaves in the same manner. Accordingly, the public discourse that posits satisfaction of

a "Black Agenda" as *the* criterion to judge the success of the
Obama presidency is misdirected. It also seems to be a waste
of considerable intellect by African American scholars, leaders, and media personalities that could be used more con-
structively during Obama's time in office. Martin would
likely conclude, as I have, that President Obama is most
likely to be the first politician with the potential to bring
about fundamental and transformational change on the his-
torically pervasive issue of race in America. Martin would
undoubtedly note the historic irony that Barack Obama, a
political leader who is neither white nor from the South,
with a substantial voter mandate of support, may be able to
rise above the old established "race relations" paradigm of
the twentieth century and chart a new direction for our
country.

Even in this light, however, Obama is first and foremost
a political leader, not a moral one. I make no judgments
about how accurate the president's moral compass may be; I
only point out that political expediencies trump moral forti-
tude in the presidency every time. What is absent from the
landscape is not a group of people like the ones who comprised the foot soldiers of The Movement but someone to
spur that group to action.

In our Web-enabled information age, it seems we can all
connect with one another to find a group with common interests. I cannot *begin* tell you what the March on Washington would have looked like if we had had today's mobile

technology to work with. But despite the many concerned people out there, history shows that the masses need someone to follow. Someone extraordinary. Where is today's Martin Luther King? I will grant that the struggles The Movement faced in the 1950s and 1960s were active and institutionalized—a big target—whereas today's racism is a bit more like an undercurrent. That makes mobilization hard. But when young people come up to me often and tell me how exciting it must have been to be in the thick of things, saying how they regret missing all the action, I always think, it's your turn to make some action. The missing ingredient is not racism; sadly, it is the leadership that can point to a better tomorrow.

The 1965 Voting Rights Act sparked the fires of subsequent black voter registration and increased voting participation that dramatically altered the political landscape of America. It was this legislative foundation that fostered and facilitated the political possibility of a successful Obama candidacy for president.

But beyond legislative measures, I would be remiss if I didn't underscore the fact that President Barack Obama's election would not have been possible without the transformative struggle, sweat, sacrifice, and tears of those in the Civil Rights Movement who believed in and hoped for Martin's "Dream." Without Dr. King's action, leadership, and legacy in dismantling segregation and institutional racism throughout the country, there would be no Barack Obama as we know him. It was not by coincidence that the president accepted the Democratic Party's nomination on the forty-fifth anniversary of the March on Washington.

Today, there are more African American officials elected to local political offices in Mississippi than in any other state in our country, with black mayors in Jackson, Greenwood, and Philadelphia (infamous venue of the murder of three civil rights workers, James Chaney, Andrew Goodman, and Michael Schwerner). This says to me that the people who once would have marched and fought for a better life for their black brothers and sisters are now holding positions in the government ranks. It's satisfying in one way: Just look at the jobs they hold. And civil service can be a noble calling. But in another way it's disheartening, because far too many of the potential leaders of the "New Movement" have become part of the status quo rather than a challenge to it.

Finally, no index of the reality of progress by African Americans—and indeed of our nation—is more sobering than an examination of our incarceration system. In his celebrated 1866 classic *Crime and Punishment*, Fyodor Dostoyevsky wrote, "The degree of civilization in a society can be judged by entering its prisons."

The United States constitutes five percent of the world's population. Yet we have 25 percent of the world's prisoners. Today there are 2.3 million Americans in jail.

African Americans represent 12 percent of our population, yet now comprise 40 percent of those in prison. Spending on penal institutions amount to roughly $77 billion per year. These facts contravene everything that Dr. King dreamed of for our country.

My wish for every reader of this book—whatever your skin color, whatever your age, whatever your religion, whatever your burdens—is for you to remember and believe that nothing is set in stone. Change can happen, and knowing that is empowering. Trust me, I've seen it firsthand. I've lived through King's Birmingham Jail and Obama's Grant Park. That covers a lot of ground in the change department.

I was once a man who did not want his life disrupted with other people's problems. But other people's problems are really the whole world's problems. And if we suffer and struggle as individuals, not units of people sorted by race or income or anything else so arbitrary, we can find solutions as individuals. This may at first glance seem to conflict with The Movement, but a deeper look reveals the truth: The Movement was a series of people joining together, crystallizing and galvanizing into a whole greater than the sum of its parts.

Change *can* happen. If you truly take that fact to heart, almost without noticing or choosing so, you'll find you are the one helping make the change.

DREAM ON,
MARCH ON . . .

Photo courtesy National Archives

In July 2010, I received a welcome offer from the United States Commission on Civil Rights to participate as a panelist and speaker at their national conference, entitled *A New Era: Defining Civil Rights in the 21st Century*. The letter of invitation read:

> We have reached a critical juncture in civil rights that necessitates an open and frank discussion about lingering racial disparities, how best to address and alleviate them, and who—whether government, civil society, the affected persons themselves, or some combination thereof—is best positioned to do so.

The Commission accurately describes the principal post-"Dream" challenges facing our current generation of civil rights and political leadership. Nevertheless, I remain hopeful and optimistic about the potential opportunities to conquer these challenges.

Martin Luther King, Jr.'s dream was nothing short of an American awakening. But the nation did not snap fully awake immediately. It has been a slow, drowsy process of pulling the reality in line with the "Dream." Yes, progress has been made. I'm not talking about the significant achievements of the many African Americans reaching the highest levels of business and politics. Rather, I am referring to the growing number of everyday Americans who effortlessly see past the color of one another's skin.

Watch television on any weekend during the college and professional football season. Players on the field and people attending the games constitute a racial mosaic of America. Whether at the universities of Mississippi, Alabama, Georgia, Syracuse, or professional teams from Oakland, Denver, Indianapolis, Baltimore, or New Orleans, the "sons of former slaves and slave owners" are "sitting down at the table of brotherhood" for all the world to see. That seems a stronger indication of our potential to get past race as a social issue than, say, the confirmation of Clarence Thomas to the Supreme Court.

Much progress has indeed been made. As an American and as a participant in the Civil Rights Movement, I'm tremendously proud of that progress. But as long as there is necessity for such a legal category as *hate crime,* the "Dream" remains unfulfilled. As long as there are patrol cops pulling over African Americans because they're driving cars considered out of their financial reach, the "Dream" remains diluted. And as long as people are selling their houses because too many black families have moved in, the "Dream" remains tarnished.

On that Super Tuesday in 2008 with Barack Obama not necessarily a sure thing but a serious candidate, my coauthor,

Stuart, actually asked me two questions in a row. I've mentioned the first already: Did you ever think you'd live to see
the day this would be happening for an African American?

Without hesitation, the answer: No.

And then: *Would it be happening if Barack Obama had
darker skin?*

Again, without hesitation, the answer: *No.*

For as long as my answer remains the truth in America,
the "Dream" Martin Luther King, Jr., brought to us remains
at least slightly out of reach.

Yet still we grasp.

In loving tribute to Stanley David Levison

In memory of James Chaney, Andrew Goodman, and Michael Schwerner, the three civil rights workers who lost their lives in Philadelphia, Mississippi, on June 21, 1964, and Addie Mae Collins, Carole Robertson, Cynthia Wesley, and Denise McNair, the young girls who died in the bombing of the 16th Street Baptist Church on September 15, 1963.

ACKNOWLEDGMENTS

The authors wish to thank the following for their support and assistance in bringing *Behind the Dream* to life:

Dr. Clayborne Carson, director of Stanford University's Martin Luther King, Jr., Institute for Research and Education, Associate Directors Tenisha Armstrong, Dr. Susan Englander, and staff Susan Carson, Regina Covington, Jane Abbott, Ashni Mohnot, Stacey Zwald, Alex Marquand-Willse, and David Lai.

Special thanks to the management and staff of the New York accounting and consulting firm of Marks, Paneth & Shron, LLP, for their technical support and the generous use of their offices.

Thanks to Carol Mann, Charles Harris, and Ron Gillyard.

And thank you for the hard work to our editor Alessandra Bastagli, along with Colleen Lawrie, Donna Cherry, and all at Palgrave, and to Andrew Berry at Letra Libre.

Clarence B. Jones offers special thanks:

To my Palo Alto friend and business colleague Carol Sands, and for the inspiration of my friends in the monthly "Think Tank" luncheon group under the leadership of Hugh C. Burroughs, Harry Bremond, Harold Boyd, and Roy Clay, Sr.

To my California extended family of Carl and Jean Dickerson, Jamie Mount, Clarence and Jackie Avant, Anthony Browne and Margo Davis, Shellye Archambeau and Scotty Scott, Harold and Sarah Boyd, Clay and Susan Carson for their loving support, inspiration and friendship. And to my New York, Washington, D.C., and Chicago extended family and friends: Michael Flicker and Annette Stauning, Joyce Johnson-Miller, James Mitchell, Jr., Leon Kassman, Raymond L. McGuire, Dan and Myra Addison, Richard Kronthal, Betsy and Richard Steenberg, Mariel Clemensen, Bennett J. Johnson and Cathy Johnson, Voza Rivers, Jamal Joseph, Lainie Cooke, Marsha Owens, John Edmonds, Gladys and Chester Redhead, and Clementine Pugh.

Special gratitude for the inspiration and friendship of Dr. Frank Greene, who passed away December 2009, for showing me the potential use of technology in support of the pursuit of educational excellence.

Special remembrance and thanks for the love and friendship of two lifelong friends, Percy Ellis Sutton and George Douglas Pugh, who passed away in 2009 and 2010, respectively; both of whom spent their lives trying to realize Dr. King's "Dream."

This book would not have been possible without the love, friendship, support and guidance of Steve Baum, Managing Partner Emeritus, Marks, Paneth & Shron and Lin Walters—my Significant Other—and the patience, literary skills, and devotion of Stuart Connelly.

Special thanks to Howard Scher, MD, New York Memorial Sloan Kettering Cancer Center and Drs. Edward Anderson and Halsted Holman of Palo Alto, CA, without whose medical supervision I may have not been able to write this book.

To those students seeking a Master Degree in Liberal Arts who enrolled in my course "From Slavery to Obama": As part of that successor generation who are beneficiaries of the "Dream" of Dr. King, they are living testament to the power of his legacy. I am indebted to their inspiration and dedication.

To Andrew Levison, who keeps the fire burning.

And to my children, Felicia, Dana, Ben, Alexia, and Tina, with love.

Stuart Connelly offers special thanks:

To those who generously helped clear copyrighted material for *Behind The Dream,* sharing their time and/or intellectual property: Billy Bragg; Peter Jenner at Sincere Management; Carol King at Chrysalis; Alex Winter at Hake's Collectibles; and Julie Cornwell at The E.W. Scripps Company.

Thank you to my literary managers, Ken Atchity and Chi-Li Wong at AEI, who've kept the faith for some time now.

Thank you Mary Jo Barthmaier, Bill Rapp, Nancy Nigrosh, Kate Barthmaier, Isaiah Washington, Sarah Copp, Paul Barthmaier, and Matt Bennett for the thoughtful and always-appreciated advice and assistance all along the way.

I will always be grateful to the other John Keats, for setting the example.

And finally, a heartfelt thank you to Clarence B. Jones—Clarence, you shared your history and memories with me as if we've known each other for a lifetime. It is a privilege to call you a collaborator and friend.

NOTES

CHAPTER ONE   HISTORY IN THE MAKING

1. In early 1963 I introduced Martin to Harry Wachtel, who was, at the time of The March, planning taking on many advisory roles and would grow to become extremely close to Martin as well.

2. All FBI wiretap transcriptions and official memorandums regarding March planning can be found in the FBI's complete file on me, Bureau File No. 100–407018. It is available through the U.S. Freedom of Information Act. A copy also resides at Stanford University's Martin Luther King, Jr. Research and Education Institute.

3. Evers was shot by Byron De La Beckwith in his driveway returning home from an NAACP meeting. De La Beckwith was tried twice in 1964 with two all-Caucasian juries deadlocked both times, but a third trial thirty years later gained a conviction. Evers is buried in Arlington National Cemetery.

4. President John F. Kennedy, in a June 22, 1963, meeting with Martin and other civil rights leaders in the Cabinet Room of the White House, cited in Arthur M. Schlesinger, *Robert Kennedy and His Times* (Boston: Houghton Mifflin, 1978), p. 349. This meeting took place immediately prior to the personal chat Kennedy had with Martin in the Rose Garden wherein he divulged that the government knew about Stanley's supposed communist ties.

5. In the 1976 report of the United States Senate Select Committee to Study Governmental Operations with Respect to Intelligence Activity, popularly known as the Church Report, the attorney general quotes the lead investigator's conclusions regarding the FBI's surveillance of Martin: "We have found that the FBI undertook a systematic program of harassment of Martin Luther King, by means both legal and illegal, in order to discredit him and harm both him and the movement he led."

   In their book, *The Lawless State* (New York: Penguin, 1976), authors Morton Halperin, Jerry Berman, Robert Borosage, and Christine Marwick assert "the most vicious FBI attack was reserved for King and the Southern Christian Leadership Conference. All of the arbitrary power and lawless tactics that had accumulated in the bureau over the years were marshaled to destroy King's reputation and the movement he led. The FBI relied on its vague authority to investigate 'subversives' to spy on King and SCLC; its vague authority to conduct warrantless wiretapping and microphonic surveillance to tap and bug him; its secrecy to conduct covert operations against him. The campaign began with his rise to leadership and grew more vicious as he reached the height of his power."

6. In Steven Kasher's book (with Myrlie Evers Williams), *The Civil Rights Movement: A Photographic History, 1954–68* (New York: Abbeville Press, 1996), the point is

confronted head-on: "Hoover's baseless suspicions about Dr. King, his virulent at-tacks on him, and his repeated attempts to destroy his reputation with the Kennedys were spurred by racist animosities and other pathological problems."

7.   In a letter to Dr. King from African American Congressman Charles Diggs (D-MI) dated June 27, 1963, both Capitol Hill fears and intimidation tactics are on clear dis-play: "There are certain limitations upon any demonstrations in the Nation's Capi-tol [sic] . . . imposed, as a result of unfortunate incidents in the past, to preserve the dignity of the Federal Government and to protect its branches from threats and in-timidation." "You would be dealing with Members of Congress indifferent to such pressure. . . ." "Can we be assured disciplinary problems will be minimized?" "A tremendous logistics problem would arise. . . ." "Would it be prudent to spend such a large sum in view of unpredictable dividends?"

8.   Jack Eisen, *The Washington Post*, August 18, 1963; also referenced in Nick Bryant, *The Bystander: John F. Kennedy and the Struggle for Black Equality* (New York: Basic Books, 2006), p. 4.

9.   Even after the unanimous Supreme Court decision in *Brown v. Board of Education* in 1954, nearly ten years later in the month of The March, only 1.18 percent of black children attended integrated schools.

10.   In the end, the group would end up renting cars and chartering buses, planes, and, in fact, twenty-one trains.

11.   Millie Floyd, *The Afro-American*, August 17, 1963, in a letter to the editor: "For many years here in Georgia, we have had a saying that the South will be integrated before the North will. . . . I am very interested to see which region, the North or the South, will send more demonstrators to the Aug. 28 March on Washington. I think the South will—and that will prove the colored Southerners are much more determined to be free than the Northerners.

   "After all, down here, we are risking death in order to register; in most North-ern towns, colored persons who are registered won't even vote."

12.   When Martin was indicted by the State of Alabama for criminal perjury and tax evasion in February 1960, Harry, Bayard Rustin, and Stanley Levison drafted the text of a full-page ad published in *The New York Times* appealing for funds to contribute to the cost of his legal defense. Dr. King's search for legal assistance in defense of this tax case was the basis for my first meeting with him at my home in California in late February of that year.

13.   A more detailed description of my first meeting with Dr. King in 1960 can be found in the introductory chapter of my book *What Would Martin Say?* (New York: HarperCollins, 2008).

14.   Bryant, *The Bystander*, p. 431, and Richard Gid Powers, *Secrecy and Power: The Life of J. Edgar Hoover* (New York: Free Press, 1988), p. 382.

15.   Though I did not have the actual wiretap transcripts in hand until years later, it was clear by the conversation that JFK had with Martin that the government was getting their information somehow. We became extremely careful when talking about Stan-ley never to use his name. Between Martin and me, he was simply "our friend."

   But under FBI surveillance, the Kennedy Administration knew Martin was still getting assistance from Stanley, even if we didn't name him. When the attorney gen-eral confronted Martin on this end-around (my speaking to Stanley and then pass-ing the information on to Martin) they tried to force him to demand that *I* sever all contact with Stanley as well. Martin refused.

16. Years later I had to grin to myself when I picked up a copy of the collection *The Covenant with Black America* (Chicago: Third World Press, 2006). In his introduction, Tavis Smiley highlights the same story forty years later! It certainly has as much to say about the political system today as it did for the 1960s.

17. Excerpt from Frederick Douglass, "West India Emancipation" speech, delivered on August 3, 1857, in Canandaigua, New York. Douglass said:

> *If there is no struggle there is no progress. Those who profess to favor freedom and yet deprecate agitation are men who want crops without plowing up the ground; they want rain without thunder and lightning. They want the ocean without the awful roar of its many waters.*
>
> *This struggle may be a moral one, or it may be a physical one, and it may be both moral and physical, but it must be a struggle. Power concedes nothing without a demand. It never did and it never will. Find out just what any people will quietly submit to and you have found out the exact measure of injustice and wrong which will be imposed upon them, and these will continue till they are resisted with either words or blows, or with both.*

CHAPTER TWO   TUESDAY

1. From the *original* text of John Lewis' proposed speech at The March. It also was a frequently used sound bite at Lewis' pre-march press conferences.

2. Ibid.

3. When Martin was in jail in Birmingham for protesting segregation in the city's department stores and public accommodations, a full-page ad appeared in *The Birmingham Herald* newspaper. The ad, headlined "A Call for Unity," was a letter published on April 12, 1963, by eight white clergymen local to Birmingham, Alabama. The writers urged an end to the Negro demonstrations "directed and led in part by outsiders" (Dr. King) that were taking place at the time, recommending that Negroes "engage in local negotiations and use the courts if rights are being denied." Martin wrote his response to the ad in the form of the "Letter from a Birmingham Jail."

4. John Lewis' speech was published in its entirety in his book (written with Michael D'Orso) *Walking with the Wind* (New York: Simon & Schuster, 1998).

5. The challenge to use sit-ins to get arrested, fill the jails, and bring the city to a standstill roused many supporters, but there was always the tacit understanding that the SCLC would bail out anyone who could not or should not stay in jail. That included many school-age boys and girls. The city, in its effort to deter the Birmingham campaign, quadrupled the cost of bail, effectively using economic terrorism to prevent the SCLC from honoring its commitments. Martin had the choice to travel the country raising bail money or lead another protest that would be sure to get him arrested. He chose the latter.

6. *The Birmingham Herald,* April 12, 1963.

CHAPTER THREE   WEDNESDAY

1. Nan Robertson, "Civil Rights Leaders Urge Proud and Orderly March," *The New York Times,* August 26, 1963.

2. Ibid.

3. Kasher, *The Civil Rights Movement,* p. 117.

4. Excerpt from the joint statement signed and issued by organizers of the MOW:

    > The Washington March of August 28th is more than just a demonstration. It
    > was conceived as an outpouring of the deep feelings of millions of white and
    > colored American citizens that the time has come for the government of the
    > United States of America, and particularly for the Congress of the government,
    > to grant and guarantee complete equality in citizenship to the Negro minority
    > of our population. As such, the Washington March is a living petition—in the
    > flesh—of the scores of thousands of citizens of both races who will be present
    > from all parts of the country. *It will be orderly, but not subservient. It will be
    > proud, but not arrogant. It will be non-violent, but not timid. It will be unified in
    > purposes and behavior, not splintered in to groups and individual competitors. It will
    > be outspoken, but not raucous.* It will have the dignity befitting a demonstration
    > in behalf of the human rights of twenty millions of people, with the eye and
    > judgment of the world focused upon Washington, D.C. on August 28th, 1963.

5. Kasher, *The Civil Rights Movement,* p. 117.
6. In the introduction to *The Bystander,* Bryant relates that the sound system rigging
    was the brainchild of Nicholas Katzenbach, RFK's deputy attorney general. Katzen-
    bach was concerned that a group of subversives, Nation of Islam or communist in-
    filtrators, might "seize control of the public address system and incite the crowd." p.
    5.
7. Kasher, *The Civil Rights Movement,* p. 117.
8. As described in the charming young reader's book by Bianca Dumas, *Robert Parris
    Moses* (Chicago: Raintree, 2004), p. 16, a part of the African American Biographies
    series.
9. Bayard Rustin, *Organizing Manual No. 1* (New York: self-published, 1963), p. 10.
10. Kasher, *The Civil Rights Movement,* p. 117.
11. We were able to get Marian Anderson worked into the program later. She sang "He's
    Got the Whole World in His Hands" beautifully.
12. Kasher, *The Civil Rights Movement,* p. 120.
13. Doris E. Saunders, ed., *The Day They Marched,* introduction by Lerone Bennett, Jr.
    (Chicago: Johnson Publishing, 1963).
14. Coretta Scott King, *My Life with Martin Luther King, Jr.* (Dallas: Holt, Rinehart
    and Winston, 1969), p. 236.
15. Ibid.
16. Mrs. King also writes that while working on his speech on the eve of The March
    Martin would call out to her for a word to clarify a thought, but she would not even
    give herself any credit for that kind of assistance, saying that mostly Martin would
    wind up using his own word. This is part and parcel of a disturbing trend I have seen
    growing over the years since his death. Those with direct interests in Martin's legacy
    do not allow for the concept of anyone truly assisting the man. For the most part,
    even the people he left behind who know better go along with this assertion. From
    the family's perspective, I imagine it's viewed as a slippery slope problem: The con-
    cern that any third-party suggestion of contribution to Martin's works will lead in-
    exorably to a concern that "ownership" claims will follow.

    It is important, then, for me to clarify: Any and all work, research, and prepa-
    ration of suggested text of speeches or articles by Stanley Levison and/or myself for
    Martin's use was, *in each and every instance,* considered to be the sole work product

of Martin. We did not then, nor do we now, claim proprietorship or "ownership" of any of the assistance we provided. We did so out of our love, respect, and devotion to Martin and his extraordinary leadership.

My wish is not for possession or credit, but that a clear account of the amazing event that was the March on Washington exists for future generations. In that context, it is important for posterity that the record is clear on Dr. King's reliance on draft speechwriters. One doesn't need to take my word for it. The FBI files on both me and Stanley Levison illustrate the fact that this was an ordinary occurrence. They are replete with transcripts of numerous wiretaps of references to our writing of letters and drafts of articles, speeches, and memos for Dr. King. A typical notation reads as follows: "On October 22, 1963, the first confidential source furnished information which indicated on that date, Miss MacDonald, King's secretary, told Jones that the speech had been received and that she had read it to King. She said that King would like two or three additional paragraphs on the present civil rights legislation concerning whether they should support a stronger or weaker bill. Jones said he would work on it."

Some of my more extensive editorial contributions can be found in my preparation of the 75-page memorandum submitted to President Kennedy by Dr. King and under his name in September 1962 in support of the SCLC's request for JFK to issue a "Second Emancipation Proclamation" and my preparation of Dr. King's speech to the 1964 Republican National Convention Platform Committee in San Francisco. There are multiple FBI memos that back up the origins of each of these written documents. Yet it is a regrettable sign of the times that, in a book seeking to celebrate the unique greatness of Dr. King, we should feel such third-party authentication of my labor of love (as well as that of Stanley Levison) is crucial.

17. Edward M. Kennedy, *True Compass: A Memoir* (New York: Twelve/Hachette Books) pp. 200–201.
18. William Cowper, "God Moves In Mysterious Ways," 1774.
19. Kennedy, *True Compass*, p. 201.
20. Russell Baker, "Capital is Occupied by a Gentle Army," *The New York Times*, August 29, 1963.

CHAPTER FOUR   A STRIKE OF LIGHTNING, THEN . . . ROLLING THUNDER

1. This was a judgment that Martin, Stanley, I, and other advisors came to at that time based not only on JFK's demeanor at the post-March Cabinet Room meeting. As one of Martin's close political advisors, either singly or together with him, after careful collective analysis and evaluation, I often rendered such political opinions, which in turn led to next-step strategies.
2. Kasher, *The Civil Rights Movement*, p. 120.
3. Malcolm X (with Alex Haley), *The Autobiography of Malcolm X* (New York: Random House, 1965), pp. 278, 280–281.
4. United States District Court for the Southern District of New York: Martin Luther KING, Jr., Plaintiff, v. MISTER MAESTRO, INC., and 20th Century-Fox Record Corporation, Defendants 224 F. Supp. 101; 1963 U.S. Dist. LEXIS 10069; 140 U.S.P.Q. (BNA) 366, December 13, 1963.
5. Clayborne Carson has said in the past that he originally experienced the March on Washington as an "epiphany," but started reconsidering soon thereafter. During

some long conversations with Stokely Carmichael, Stokely's suggestion that The March represented a "sanitized version" of the true racial struggle made sense to him.

In 2010, Clay told me, "My first conversation with Stokely actually took place in the days before The March, when I met him at the annual meeting of the National Student Association (NSA). He encouraged me to work with SNCC in the Deep South, but, at that point in my life, going to The March marked the boundaries of my 'militancy.' My involvement later grew much deeper as I became more aware of people like Stokely, with whom I would interact for the rest of his life."

As he is now the executive director of the King Research and Education Institute, obviously Clay has come full circle with respect to his feelings about Dr. King's power while still maintaining his understanding of the more militant aspects of the racial struggle. In recent years he has compared The Movement to Exodus, saying, "If no one had told the Exodus stories, it would not have inspired people throughout the world for thousands of years."

CHAPTER FIVE   IN THE PRESENT, TENSE

1. That understanding is in part why I ended up, only a few short years after Martin's assassination, as the co-owner, publisher, and editor of *The New York Amsterdam News*, then the country's largest African American–oriented weekly newspaper.

2. One memorable moment of the conference was when Lech Walesa, leader of the Trade Union Solidarity Movement from Gdansk, Poland, took and held my hand. Speaking through his translator, Piotr Gulczynski, and looking directly into my eyes, he said, "We watched television and saw and heard your Dr. King and his followers sing 'We Shall Overcome.' We memorized the words, even though we did not speak English. When Solidarity went on strike, thousands of our members would sing 'We Shall Overcome' to the authorities. That's how much we loved and respected Dr. King." Tears came to my eyes. I embraced Lech and thanked him for sharing that story.

3. The story remains fascinating to me as further education in the demimonde of politics: The fact that Barack Obama would choose Joe Biden as a running mate after such a comment speaks volumes on the "strange bedfellows" conceit.

4. I commend the reader to the National Urban League's annual surveys of "The State of Black America" and the compilation *Covenant with Black America* (Chicago: Third World Press, 2006). They provide a wealth of information and statistical comparisons between the progress of African Americans and white Americans and Hispanics.

5. United States Government, Kerner Commission, "Report of the National Advisory Commission on Civil Disorders" (Washington: U.S. Government Printing Office, 1968).

6. Lynn A. Curtis and Fred R. Harris, "The Millennium Breach" (Washington: white paper, 1998), p. 1. The Milton S. Eisenhower Foundation is a Washington-based non-profit organization that continues the work of the Kerner Commission. Curtis, the president of foundation, worked with Harris, a former U.S. Senator (D-OK) who served on the original Kerner Commission.

7. Martin Luther King, Jr.'s speech "Transforming a Neighborhood into a Brotherhood," presented to the National Association of Real Estate Brokers at the Fairmont Hotel, August 1965.

8. Martin's stance on money is in part why it was so absurd that he was charged as a tax evader in 1960; he was the last person who would skim off the top of his government obligation.

9. *Playboy,* January 1965, interview by Alex Haley.

10. With due respect to Marilyn French (author of *The Women's Room*), Betty Friedan, Gloria Steinem, and others, it was the Civil Rights Movement under the moral and political leadership of Dr. King that most effectively spoke truth to white male power in America, especially in the government. It was Dr. King who raised America's consciousness about the unfairness and inequity of the exclusion of African Americans, contrary to the precepts of our Declaration of Independence, from employment, education, and other opportunities to participate, on an equal basis, in white male-dominated and controlled businesses, colleges, universities, and foundations. The leadership of white women, as a class, was able to utilize this platform of elevated consciousness created by Martin to effectively appeal to the white-power leadership of male-dominated businesses and private institutions to demonstrate their "exclusion" similar to that of the African American community. Statistically, a larger percentage of white women than African Americans were ready, willing, and able to walk through these new doors of opportunities as a result of their consciousness being raised by the moral appeal and leadership of Dr. King.

11. Martin Luther King, Jr., *Why We Can't Wait* (New York: Harper & Row, 1964) p.128

12. The principal barrier confronting President Johnson was the need for both houses of Congress to agree to any course of action he might propose; in addition, there was the question of whether a substantial body of domestic public opinion, at that time, would support any further proposals he would make, after passing Medicare, the Civil Rights Bill of 1964, and enacting the Voting Rights Bill of 1965.

13. Eldridge Cleaver, *Soul on Ice* (New York: McGraw-Hill, 1968), p. 83.

14. Those in attendance representing the Civil Rights Movement with me were James Baldwin, Dr. Kenneth Clark, Lena Horne, Harry Belafonte, Rip Torn, Lorraine Hansberry, and Jerome Smith from the SNCC.

15. Bill George, "Barack Obama: A Leader for the 'We' Generation," *Business Week,* November 11, 2008.

INDEX